GODLY GEMS

TO IMPACT YOUR

life

GODLY GEMS
TO IMPACT YOUR *life*

REINHARD BONNKE

CfaN CHRIST FOR ALL NATIONS

Australia • Brazil • Canada • Czech Republic • Germany • Hong Kong • Kenya • Latin America • Nigeria • New Zealand • Singapore • South Africa • United Kingdom • United States

© 2019 by Reinhard Bonnke
GODLY GEMS

Published by Christ for all Nations
PO Box 590588
Orlando, FL 32859-0588
CfaN.org

ISBN: 978-1-933446-90-5 (paperback)
ISBN: 978-1-933446-91-2 (e-book)

Editorial revisions by Rick Kern
Interior Design by Grupo Nivel Uno Inc.
Cover Design by DesignstoGo.net

Printed in the UK

Run of 6,000 copies for Free Distribution

NOT FOR RESALE

Dedication

I dedicate this book to all who hunger and thirst for the deeper truth of the Word of God. "They shall be filled." (Matt 5:6) Keep reading it — again and again, and you will be richly blessed. If you wish, you may use these "GODLY GEMS" in your home-group or church. Let the blessings radiate in your life!

Reinhard Bonnke, Evangelist

Introduction

The glory of Jesus

Nobody can take away the glory of Jesus and no time can dim it. It is there in Himself and is not produced by artificial pomp or outward circumstance. He needs no triumphalism, no trumpets, and no brilliant display. In peasant's dress, His glory breaks through. Put Him on a Cross and it can destroy nothing of Him. He triumphs over it, transforms it, turns this thing of shame and scandal into the greatest symbol of glory on earth. The ugliest instrument of human torture and hate — the cross, sticky with gore, is transfigured until a former enemy must call out, "Forbid it Lord that I should boast save in the death of Christ my Lord[1]" The more you attack Jesus, the more His mercy, his pity, His patience appears. Be His enemy, and you only give Him an opportunity to forgive, to seek, to save, and display the eternal glory of His indestructible love.

My prayer is that the glory of Jesus may shine through every word of this book and right into the heart of every reader.

Reinhard Bonnke

True Worship

ACTS OF OVERPOWERING LOVE

My eyes are glued to Matthew 26:6-13, where Mary of Bethany broke the bottle of precious ointment to anoint the Lord. The reaction of Jesus almost seems an overreaction. For such a "small service" He gave her such high honor when he said, "Assuredly, I say to you, wherever this the gospel is preached in the whole world, what this woman has done will also be told as a memorial to her." What moved Jesus so deeply? It was the striking similarity between the act of the woman and His own act. She had broken the bottle and in its broken pieces Christ saw His own body, which was about to be broken hours later. She spilled the ointment, He shed His blood — both were acts of overpowering and sublime love! She had anointed Him for His burial. He gave His "life as a ransom for many" — for the salvation of the world. That is the gospel! And this is what we preach and keep on preaching.

WORTHY IS THE LAMB

In Revelation, Chapter 4, we read of twenty-four great beings worshipping before the throne in heaven. The reason for their worship is in Verse 11. "Thou art worthy, O Lord, to receive glory and honor and power; for thou hast created all things and for thy pleasure they are and were created." However, in Chapter 5, there is a new view. Not only the twenty-four great angelic intelligences, but "ten thousand times ten thousand and thousands of thousands" worshiped, and their theme was not creation. They sang "Worthy is the Lamb that was slain." That is the truth about everything! He made all things and redeemed all things. We only know God as He makes Himself known to us. He is infinite. We don't know everything about God — only what He shows us of Himself. There are other views of God we shall never see, but this view is enough to occupy us forever. When we come together with song and praise, and if we want to join the hosts of heaven, that is their theme — the Lamb of God, not creation but the core of creation, the Lamb as it had been slain. That is Christian worship. Cross-less, bloodless worship is not Christian.

GOD IS OUR NATURAL HABITAT

Why is music so precious to so many? When we are touched by inspired music, we often receive a glimpse of the eternal. Music only suggests infinity; however, the melody echoes a faraway greatness that it cannot fulfill. That infinity is God Himself, and what music merely suggests is given to us when we receive salvation through Jesus Christ and begin to worship Him.

God is our natural habitat. In Him we live and move and have our being. (Acts 17:28) Until we hear and obey the gospel, until we find Him, we remain caged. Men and women everywhere are beating their heads against prison bars forged by their own materialism and unbelief. Their very money holds them captive. Deep calls to deep and height to height within our souls. Our art, our poetry, our works of beauty are but expressions of imprisoned creatures who dimly remember the glories of the free air and the mountains. While good in themselves, these expressions remain mere reflections of reality. Jesus is the reality behind all that we see or do. His gospel releases us from bondage, allowing us to come into our true element, our intended heritage!

TRUE NOBILITY

Christians are being thrown into jail and being tortured. But those who know Jesus Christ would rather suffer than not be with Him. Once you know Christ you can't help but talk about Him. The confessors and martyrs of Jesus are the true nobility of whom the world is not worthy. Saving our lost world is more important than the very stars the creator made. Stars will dim, but, "...those who are wise will shine, like the stars for ever and ever." "The man who does the will of God lives forever." (Dan 12:3 and Jn 2:17)

FLICKERING CANDLES

The candle flame of human genius sparkles briefly before being extinguished by the winds of time, but the lamp of God never flickers. Jeremiah said, "O Lord, I know the way of man is not in himself; it is not in man who walks to direct his own steps." (Jer 10:23) Without divine instruction, the structure of our lives collapses in chaos. This is exactly the state of those who have no knowledge of the Lord. Life for the unregenerate is a meaningless disorder. "It is God who makes my way perfect." (Ps 18:32) Walk in it.

POLISH YOUR PRAISES TO GOD

Years ago, I ministered in different churches in America. When I entered a Christian bookshop, I saw a big brass-plaque with the words "Praise the Lord." I bought and took it with me to Frankfurt, Germany, where we lived at that time and fixed it on the outside of the house. Suddenly I realized that I had installed it at the very spot where neighbors had their plaques with, "Beware of the dog." Well, Jesus is all-in-all to my family and me. Weather-beaten by storm, snow, and rain, my brass-sign lost its shine, so we polished our "Praise the Lord" and it began to shine like gold. This is a message for us all...

Gospel

ALTERNATIVE LIFE-STYLE

We don't present the gospel as an alternative lifestyle. It is not just a better way of living, it is the only way of life at all. All other ways are death ways. The Gospel is "the word of truth," not the word of happiness. God can do nothing for us, except through Jesus Christ.

THE PROPHETIC FORMULA

The prophetic formula in the Bible always was, "Thus says the Lord," not, "I am telling you!" Prophets just passed on what they had heard from God, and that was that. It was not their business to defend it or to invite questions — contention was not something they got involved in. It was the Lord's responsibility to confirm the righteousness of His own Word. He still does.

NO DUMMY AMUNITION

When a gun is loaded with blanks, the bang and recoil are the same as they would be with live ammunition. A difference can be observed in the use of live ammunition and blanks, but not in the noise. The dummy ammunition makes no mark on the target, because it never reaches it, but the real bullet can hit its mark. We are not interested in mere bang and recoil, excitement and spectacular gospel displays, even if those draw hundreds of thousands of people. We want to see something live hit the target. The crowds may come, but we must, by faith, let loose a true broadside of Holy Spirit firepower for something to be accomplished. *Preach the original gospel and you get the original results!* Multitudes are born again, lives are completely changed, churches are filled, hell is plundered, and heaven is populated.

THE EXPLOSIVE GOSPEL

A sermon may be a neatly turned and engineered presentation like the casing of an armor piercing shell, but it needs filling with explosive or it will bounce off the case-hardened minds of unbelievers. Their prejudices are fortified with argument, but the explosive power in the sermon filled with the Holy Spirit can demolish it. The gospel is always a surprise attack. It gets at men from a direction they never planned to defend. They are prepared for argument, but the gospel doesn't argue. They are prepared for sentiment, but the gospel is not sentimental. It comes with the melting waters of eternity flowing through their soul.

WHAT HAS GOD DONE FOR US?

People ask, "What has God done for me?" Well, God has done everything for us. For a start, He gave His life for us. Our every breath is a sign of His care. God is perfect and cannot forget us, He esteems us beyond price. He made us for love, for Himself, and that is why He came to save us. He wrote the contract of our redemption with a pen dipped in the blood of His own Son, and it is absolute and sure.

GOSPEL INSIGHTS

The world doesn't mind religion at all. It likes religion — but it doesn't like the gospel. If God can be relegated to the religious corner in the spiritual ghetto, all is well. God is not just religion! The gospel is not an open forum, but an open confrontation with world wickedness. The Bible is a challenge to the world system. The world system is not founded on truth, but on expedience. Its controlling factors are not related to righteousness but to what they call "business." They don't mind if you go through a few religious routines on a Sunday, but the gospel is a different thing completely. It calls for repentance and trust in Jesus. He is the only Savior, and the gospel is the power of God.

NO PEBBLES

The Bible is a solid rock, not a collection of Christian opinion-pebbles.

SUCCSESS CAN BE FAILURE

Today some churches get by without too much Holy Spirit but replace Him with general attractions. The Holy Spirit is neither prayed down nor worked up but is a gift to take. Without the Holy Spirit even our success is failure. We do not reinforce the Holy Spirit by prayer — He is omnipotent without our help. He wants to be alongside God's children. That is His call.

JUMPING TO A QUICK CONCLUSION

Two skydivers jump from a plane at 15,000 feet. Both are wearing parachutes. One of them folds his arms, ignores the ripcord, and says to himself, "I'm perfectly safe because of my parachute." He is still saying these words as he hits the ground at nearly 100 miles per hour. The other skydiver knows he will be safe only if he does something. He pulls the ripcord and lands safely. We may know about the Christian faith. We may respect Jesus and agree that what He did on the cross is the answer to our deepest needs. But until we ask for His help and commit our lives to Him, it is like falling with a closed parachute. We need to take urgent action. We need to pull the ripcord while there is still time. The ripcord is this, "Whosoever calls upon the name of the Lord shall be saved." (Rom 10:13) There is nothing else we can do. We cannot save ourselves — we can only throw ourselves on what Jesus achieved for us on the cross. He has done everything that we need. Let's act on it, or else we jump to a quick conclusion.

GOOD CHRISTAN CARGO

Preach Christ! Some preach "healing" or "power" or the "Holy Spirit" or just "God." This is all good Christian cargo to be taken on board, but the vessel is "Jesus Christ." There is nothing without Him, no healing, no power, no Holy Spirit, and not even God for, "No man comes to the Father but through Me." (Jn 14:6)

CHANGING ANCIENT CUSTOMS

The apostles were accused of changing ancient customs (see Acts 21:21), and that was indeed their intention. It was dangerous work. The apostles' work was to move a mountain — a mountain of traditions and attitudes, which over a thousand years had become the laws of nations. In fact, spreading the gospel went beyond changing ways and customs. They reshaped entire thought-patterns of those times to penetrate the hearts, souls, and minds of men and women. Twelve unlearned men. Imagine it!

Our work is not to make the gospel relevant to the world. Of course, we speak to the world in its own language. The whole idea of preaching the word is to interpret it for the understanding of modern hearers. But the old liberal idea was to adjust the gospel to the pattern of the world to make it acceptable. If the world no longer believed in the supernatural, the solution was to preach a gospel devoid of the supernatural. This was a betrayal of the Christian message. We cannot compromise! To change the world, we must be different from the world. We must challenge what people think. If they don't believe, we do not adjust to their unbelief. "Hallelujah to the cross, it shall never suffer loss."

PREACH JESUS!

When people go to church, they want Jesus. Not politics. Not sentimentalism. Not the "stranger of Galilee" as a distant, ideal figure. They don't want a phantom, a myth. If they have read the Bible, they want to meet that same Jesus in all His glorious vitality. Who wouldn't? Preach *that* Jesus, and the

Holy Spirit is bound to reveal Him. He will step into the midst of the crowd, just as He promised.

WHAT HOLDS THE TWO TESTAMENTS TOGETHER?

The Old Testament and New Testament in the Bible are closely linked. We would never understand the whole truth of Christianity without the Old Testament. We Christians do not Hebrew-ize the New Testament, but we Christianize the Old Testament. This is because only through Jesus Christ can the Old Testament be understood. With Him everything falls into place. *He* is "The Word" that became flesh (Jn 1:14), and "He is before all things, and in Him all things hold together." (Col 1:17) That is Jesus, the One we love.

THE KINGDOM OF GOD IS NEAR

Jesus did not preach repentance by saying, "Hell is near," but, "Repent because the Kingdom of God is near." One threatens an enemy but warns a friend. Jesus never threatened sinners but warned them. Romans 2:4 says, "The goodness of God leads you to repentance." Repentance should not be preached threateningly but as a gift.

MAN-MADE RELIGIONS

Manmade religions all have the same mark — they consist of what people must *do*. They all have elaborate systems, duties to be carried out, and ceremonies to be observed, laws about this and that. That is religion. But Christianity is totally different. It is not a system of religious observances. It consists of *what God does for us!* False gods need to be carried, but the God of the Bible carries His people (Is 46:1). In the same chapter we read of God saying, "Listen to me... I have made you and I will carry you; I will sustain you and I will rescue you." Religion is a car without an engine that you must push. The gospel is a car with an engine. Get in and ride, you will surely arrive.

NEVER PERISH

The Bible never speaks of the Christian faith as only a belief system, but always as the instrument of new resources. Basically, Christianity is the release of the Holy Spirit into the world. Faith itself is not power, but the link to power. 2 Peter 1:4 says we are, "partakers of the divine nature," that can never change, which fills believers forever. Jesus said, "I give (my sheep) eternal life and they shall never perish." (Jn 10:28)

OUR MESSAGE IS JESUS

Christians have only one thing to boast about: *a crucified redeemer!* That's our gospel. Our message is *Jesus* — not success, music, academic brilliance, politics, and church buildings. It is *Jesus.* Any success that does not stem from the gospel of Christ crucified is false success. Any song that has no relation to His cross, is an empty jingle.

MANPOWER ARMED WITH GOD'S POWER

The whole, simple Christian agenda is "Operation Save." It is total mobilization of all resources for an all-out world-war against unbelief and the devil. It is manpower armed with God's power. "You will receive power," Jesus promised in Acts 1:8, and He kept His promise. Immediately after that Peter could say, "We are all witnesses." Let's be part of this "Operation Save."

SOCIAL GOSPEL

The "Social Gospel" is a gospel of self-help, not divine help. No social scheme carries God's power — only the gospel. The gospel puts the spirit of generosity, righteousness, and unselfishness within people, like music in a musician.

ETERNAL LIFE

The Bible speaks of "the ages of the ages," the "eons of the eons" (Gal 1:5), because neither Greek nor Hebrew had a word like ours for eternity. However, it does speak of God being changeless, having neither beginning nor ending, the One from whom all things have their origin. "Eternal life," means His life, which is uncreated and undiminishing. To be in Christ means we live with Him. He never becomes any older, and the quality of His life becomes ours. Our life span moves into His and we can truly say that we have "eternal life." What a gift!

IMMUNE TO CRITICISM

Let's not be man-pleasers but God-pleasers. He who is immune to the praise of man is also immune to the criticism of man. Let the Lord be your glory and the lifter of your head. (Ps 3:3)

NEW OWNERSHIP

When you become a Christian the ownership of your life changes hands. In the past, you were the boss, doing things in the way you saw best. For many people, this meant looking after themselves above everything else. But now you have a new boss, you have given your life to Jesus Christ. This is what it means to be a Christian — Jesus is now in charge, as the Lord of your life. The Apostle Paul said, "If you confess with your mouth, Jesus is Lord, and believe in your heart that God raised him from the dead, you will be saved." (Rom 10:9) What does this mean in practice? It means a new way of life. As we submit our lives to God and become His servants, we find an amazing new freedom. We are no longer the slaves of sin, but instead, we are free to do good. As Jesus said, "I have come that they may have life and have it to the full." (Jn 10:10) We start to live out the life of what Jesus called "the Kingdom of God." In simple terms, this means accepting that God rules us as our King. Jesus spoke about this way of life in His famous "Sermon on the Mount," which you can find in Matthew, chapters 5 to 7. It also means keeping to the Ten Commandments found in Exodus 20:1-17. They aren't very popular today — our society has turned them into the Ten Suggestions! But these God-given rules were never intended to restrict or spoil our lives, as many people think. Instead, they act like a government health warning on a pack of cigarettes: "Doing these things can damage your life."

MORE THAN A MAN

The Roman captain knew the routine of crucifixion. (Mk 15:37-39) First the crucified criminals were spitting and cursing, then as their strength abated, death would slowly set in. Now, on horseback, the captain stood eye to eye with the dying Jesus! Then we read, "Jesus cried with a loud voice and breathed his last." That got the captain's attention, because Christ's last words from the cross were "Father into your hands I Commend my Spirit!" Jesus had cried "with a loud voice," full of energy, and had commanded His Spirit to leave His body. It happened that very same moment. Jesus did not die of a broken heart. *He died at His own command!* Long before this, the Lord had said in John 10: 17-18, "I have power to lay down my life..." And that was observed by that heathen soldier. The captain's revelation and conclusion? Jesus is more than a man! Jesus is the Son of God! Jesus is my Savior! Trust in Jesus brings peace with God!

THE GOSPEL REEVALUATES LIFE

The cross is God's tool to re-shape our purpose and meanings. The gospel is like that, we embrace it and it embraces us. It clings to us with magnetic power, leads us, takes us where love alone would ever go, to do what love alone would ever think of doing, what He, who is love wants done, if He can find somebody to do it. Can He? Will you respond?

YES OR NO — LIGHT OR NIGHT

When the servant Dumah asked the prophet Isaiah, "Watchman, what of the night?" the prophet replied, "The morning comes, and also the night." (Is 21:11-12) This was not vague; it simply pointed out that the answer was depending on Edom's response to God. If Edom turned to God, it would be day. If not, it would be night. The same principle applies today. For those whose hand is not in the hand of Jesus the landscape of tomorrow is full of fearful dangers. For those who have come to Him, their future is the land of a victorious Christ. "Take my hand, precious Lord, lead me on, let me stand..."

PLENTY OF COMPETITORS

Christianity has plenty of competitors if you rank it lower than what it is and want it to be like that — just a part-time interest, a good cause, a Sunday club, or psychological comfort for old age, all merely incidental. As someone has said, "The church is where the old close their eyes and the young eye their clothes." But that is not it. Christianity is Christ and Jesus Christ is life, the comprehensive purpose and power of life, life for the living. Nobody else, no religion big or small, has anything like that on offer, even if you search the whole globe. We need something that keeps us truly alive in a traffic jam, or when a tsunami of misfortune swamps us. Impossible? The Bible is about that "impossible," about rooting out stuffiness from the core of our being. Jesus said, "I have come that they may have life and have it more abundantly." (Jn 10:10) *Life!* That is Christianity.

APPROPRIATION OF GOD'S PROMISE BY TRUST

God promised to Moses things Moses never began to enjoy, but it had revealed God's will in the matter, and the same thing would be done but for Joshua. If God's promises apply to our situation, then they are promises as much to us, as to the original receivers... For example, Christ promised the Holy Spirit's power to His disciples to be His witnesses throughout the whole world, and until the whole world receives that witness the promise holds good. We appropriate God's promises by trust.

GREAT CHRISTIANS

Most people would like to be a great Christian, but they try it out and consequently give up. What's wrong? Simply this — we can't be a fish by diving into an aquarium. We cannot be what we are not, but we can be what we are — anywhere! Christians are God's miracles, they are not self-made. Self-made Christians are usually lousy workmanship. Yet, it is as if we all had a cell phone with God's number. "Whoever calls on the name of the Lord shall be saved." (Rom 10:13) The name of the Lord is *Jesus*. Call on Him in prayer and then it happens like the Bible says, "We are His workmanship created in Christ Jesus for good works." (Eph 2:10) You are saved!

HISTORY

Bible-history is God's summary of events. What we call history is a record colored by the writers' own outlook. Bible history is God's unspoiled view. "Your Word is truth." (Jn 17:17) The Word of God is our true and only platform. *Preach the Word!*

MOUSE WITH A MEGAPHONE

The Bible says that, "the devil is like a roaring lion." (1 Pet 5:8) He comes in the darkness and tries to frighten the children of God with his mighty roar. But when you switch on the light of the Word of God, you discover that there is no lion. There is only a mouse with a megaphone! Got it?

NOT COLD DOCTRINE

Evangelism is good news, not cold doctrine. It is a finger pointing to the living Jesus Christ, who is the same yesterday, today, and forever. (Heb 13:8) Yesterday's newspaper is history, but Jesus is the "today figure," the greatest in history, doing more and affecting more people than any other man on earth now. The press and broadcasting thrive on bad news, they do not want the gospel and leave the masses in ignorance of what Christ is doing. But He is still good news. It is left to us, people anointed by the Holy Spirit, to bring the gospel to the world — and to go on doing it. "Go into all the world and preach the gospel to all creatures." (Mk 16:15)

WATER FOR LIVING

The water supply companies don't need to research what people are like. Everybody needs their "product." The gospel is living water. No man has invented water, yet no man can live without it. We all need Jesus — even those who don't think so. Only Jesus saves, there is no other!

WHEN GOD MADE ADAM

When God made Adam, He did not ask Adam's permission. Nobody is asked if they want to be born. But we are all asked if we want to be born-again and belong to the new order. Now is the time to choose. "As many as received him to them He gives the right to be the children of God." (Jn 1:12) When Adam sinned in the Garden of Eden, God broke His day of rest, His Sabbath, and acted at once. Why? Because *He* is incapable of doing nothing as long as there is one lost soul.

NOT ALTERNATIVE BUT ULTIMATUM

The apostles never modified the gospel to avoid offending people. They preached an uncompromising, full-blooded truth. The cross is not an alternative but an ultimatum. Paul did not enter into dialogue to find some common ground of "interfaith" agreement. There was no agreement. The cross of Christ stood plainly out against the sky for Greeks and Jews alike. "Behold the Lamb of God."

GOD SEEKS US

Jesus came "to seek and to save the lost." (Lk 19:10) *God seeks us!* Amazing, His heart yearns and churns for us! The Good Shepherd leaves the 99 to seek the one straying sheep. People say that they "found the Lord," but the Lord was never lost. *He finds us.* Adam was lost, and God was the loser. But Jesus came to seek us and through Him, God is the finder — Jesus found us!

JESUS IS THE MESSAGE

It can be argued that this or that religion is better than another, but the gospel offers only one thing — *Jesus.* He is the only one opening his arms to all people. Does anyone have another Jesus to offer? He is everything, He is the Alpha and Omega. The Lord said, "He who believes in me has everlasting life." (Jn 6:47). Jesus is not a religion. He is a person to meet and live by, the living Word. He is not a messenger from God. He is "the message" and that what the messengers talked about. There is life in Him, and that life comes to us through the Word of God.

SELF-AUTHENTICATING

Bible Christians don't argue about the Bible. They rely upon its own built-in proof. It is a messenger carrying adequate credentials. It is self-authenticating. "It lives and abides forever," said the Apostle Peter. It continues to exist because it is living truth. Believers just let it live.

· Godly Gems ·

THE GOSPEL IS DIVINE

Jesus was not raised on a cross to raise our standard of living. He did not die in blood for some happy feelings, but to save us from eternal hell. God is not a heavenly social security system and the gospel no social gospel. It is a revelation about us and about Jesus Christ the Savior.

LIFE QUALITY

Paul used two (Greek) words for life, "Bios" and "Zoe." Bios is human biological life, created life. Zoe is God's own life, uncreated, called "eternal life." It is holy, and we can't compare it as like this or that. "Eternal" is a code word for a life-quality so rich that it can't die or be destroyed. Jesus said, "I give (my sheep) eternal life and they shall never perish." Believers are "partakers of the divine nature." (Jn 10:28 and 2 Pet 1:4) This "fullness" through faith is what the New Testament is mainly about.

WITHOUT THE RESURRECTION WE ARE STUCK IN "GOOD FRIDAYS"

Jesus Christ? Nobody is a "fan" of someone they know nothing about. An open mind is not to be confused with one empty of information. "Saved?" "born again?" Why should anybody want to be "saved" or "born again" unless they understand it? Seven out of ten who don't believe in the gospel don't know what it is they don't believe in! No info, no sale. People say, "I don't like it because I've never tried it." Millions do try it, however, and are interested, very much so! Jesus makes people sit up, like the young man He raised from the dead at Nain. Effort? What, to rise from the dead? To be saved? Yes, but it is Christ's effort. *Jesus saves!* What could ignorance of the gospel do for them? To know Christ and the power of His resurrection life could change their trivialized and smothered existences. Without the resurrection it's all Good Fridays.

DEBT

If we have the gospel, we owe it, we do not own it. "I am a debtor both to the Greeks, and to the Barbarians, both to the wise, and to the unwise." (Rom 1:14)

STEWARDS

We are stewards of the gospel, not its prison wardens. The steward must disburse what he controls, not lock up treasures of truth protectively out of harm's way. Exposing the gospel to its enemies defends the faith best — it is fully capable of dealing with them.

BORDER TO ETERNITY

The border to eternity is never ahead of us. It runs parallel to life and can be crossed over any day by anybody — old or young.

BECOMING AN EVENT

The gospel is news, and news does not exist unless it is communicated. There cannot be un-communicated news. The word gospel means "Good News." *It comes into existence each time you preach it.* It is an act, not a dead letter. The Good News is not a mere truth or doctrine. When you preach it, the gospel happens and becomes an event.

TREASURE CHEST

Jesus told us a parable. A merchant found one fine pearl that was worth a phenomenal amount and he sold everything else he had to raise enough money to buy it (Matt 13:45-46). This is a picture of God emptying the treasure chest of His love for us. We were no bargain. We did not look very much like a valuable jewel. Yet He took us with all our worthless baggage, rottenness, debts, nastiness, and wickedness. He drew us to Himself ignoring everything in us that was foul and corrupt. Then like a heavenly valet, He cleaned us up, gave us a complete makeover, clothed us in righteousness, girdled us with immaculate grace, and made us fit to enter the presence of the King in His beauty. That effort left Him soaked in His own sweat and blood on the trodden grass of Gethsemane. Then finally that awful hour of devilish agony, hanging like a rag nailed to a tree. "He was nailed to the cross for me…"

SURPRISED GRATITUDE

Behind Abraham's attitude was his faith that God was ordering things. He believed God's Word to him "I am your very great reward." (Gen 15:1) There was no need for him to live a life of strain and anxiety about loss or gain. If he trusted God, God's plan would work out in his affairs. He didn't want to have what God didn't want him to have. King David a thousand years later found the same truth. He adopted Abraham's outlook and enjoyed the great advantage of letting God take over. He wrote a song of surprised gratitude (2 Sam 23) and described God's plan for him in his house as being "ordered in all things and sure" (v 5). Jesus put the principle of Abraham into His famous promise of the Sermon on the Mount found in Matthew 6:33, "Seek first the Kingdom God and his righteousness and all these things will be given you as well." He said "Don't worry about your life. Do not worry about tomorrow."

THE POWER OF LOVE

Christ's death was His greatest achievement and God's greatest act. The power of love conquered the love of power. It was no mistake, no misfortune, and no accident. Christ was not a martyred victim, but a mighty victor, our champion and God's hero. The Father in heaven sent Him to hunt out and destroy the devil and evil. A greater David faced a huge Goliath. The Son of God overthrew our greatest enemy, sin, and our final foe, death. The world ran true to form when it crucified Christ. God also ran true to form in what He did about it. He turned red blood into royal redemption. Men took a lovely tree, stripped it, and twisted it into the stark beams of the cross. It was their logo of hate. Christ picked it up, stained it with His life's blood, and gave it back to us — His logo of love. He invested that tree with a glory it never had before. Its wood became a door of hope and made us worth all that we cost. O, how I love Jesus...

WHEN JESUS CAME TO EARTH

Jesus came down to earth — He breached the barrier between human beings and God and touched the untouchables. His coming raised the share value of human beings to infinity. We are the most valuable creatures that God ever made because we cost God His Son, who willingly sacrificed Himself for us. God lavished "His great love" on us. (Eph 2:4) That "great love" is not an emotion but a person, His Son — God loved us through and with Him. What else could we ask for, what higher tribute can we pay ourselves than to take Jesus into our lives? "What is man that you are mindful of him, the son of man, that you care for him?" (Ps 8:4)

TIME DOES NOT TURN WRONG TO RIGHT

A very old religion isn't right because it is very old. Its age proves nothing if it is true or not. The idea that the earth is flat is very old — but it is also wrong! A forged painting, which is 1000 years old, is still a fake! Time doesn't turn a counterfeit into an original. Wrong stays wrong forever. The gospel is also old, but because it was true in the beginning it remains true today. Jesus saves!

OLD AND COLD?

A young man said to me "I am 17 years-old, and the Bible is 2000, I don't want to live by such antique rules, I want to be modern." I told him that the sun is much older than 2000 years, yet I never heard anybody say, "I am cold because the sun is old!" The sun is old but hot, the Bible is old but powerful!"

THE CHRIST WE SERVE

Christianity has an unconditional "Welcome" above its doors for the storm tossed, the broken in spirit, and the inadequate. It is the arm of God's love thrown around those who have given up on themselves, or been given up by the world, and have not got what it takes. If you would believe you would see the glory of God (Jn 11:40). Christ can make us — we who otherwise would never make it. In the Gospels, we see Him coming open-faced and open-armed. To Him, there were no nobodies, nor riffraff, no social rejects. He came for lost sheep. To women, who were treated as subspecies in some eastern countries, even as they are now, Christ gave honor. This *is* the Christ we serve. This *is* Christianity.

DIVINE HUMOR

Divine humor! I smile when I read Acts, Chapter 5. The High Priest and Sadducees laid hands on the apostles for preaching that Jesus had risen from the dead. They threw them into the public jail for the night. In the morning the nation's rulers brought the whole ruling body together to deal with these Jesus preachers. They sat in pompous importance waiting for the guards to drag the cowed apostles into court. But they came back without them. The prisoners had vanished under their noses. Consternation! "...a powerful hand from God..." had unlocked their prison. Furious and frustrated the authorities could only put on a show of violence and threats. The Bible's final touch of humor is that, "The apostles never stopped teaching and proclaiming the good news that Jesus is the Christ." (Acts 5:42) Christians never have stopped, and never will stop. We obey God more than man.

THE STARTING PISTOL

When I was a young missionary in Africa, I had an office to look after. The monthly rent was only about $50, but one day I could not pay, and I prayed and groaned all day, "Dear Lord, send me somehow $50 to pay the rent." The hours passed, evening came, but I still had no money. Slowly, I walked down the road to the house where we stayed as a family. Suddenly, in the middle of that road, the power of the Lord came upon me. I heard His voice clearly in my heart, "Do you want Me to give you one million dollars?" One million dollars! My heart raced. What I could do with that amount of money! Why, with a million dollars I could bombard the whole world with the gospel, I thought. But then, a different thought struck me. I am not at all a weepy man, but tears began running down my face, and I cried, "No, Lord, I am not asking for one million dollars. I want more than that. I am asking for one million souls! One million souls less in hell and one million more in heaven — that shall be the purpose of my life and ministry." That moment I heard the Holy Spirit whispering in my very spirit, words I had never heard or read, "You will plunder hell and populate heaven for Calvary's sake." That day, a determination gripped me. I knew that God had greater plans for my life, and I set out to fulfill them in progressive stages. God has granted me ever increasing blessing and grace. How often since then have I seen the devastating power of the gospel crash against the gates of hell, storming the dark domains of Satan! I have often seen, within one week, over a million precious people respond to the call of salvation in our gospel campaigns. I joked with my co-workers that, "If Jesus keeps on saving souls at this rate, one day the devil is going to sit alone in hell." I am glad to make Satan sorry. Knowing the power of the gospel, we do not need to be anxious. Jesus is more than sufficient for every need. The world is sick, and Jesus has the only remedy — the gospel. Our part is simply that we must carry this medicine to the patients. Christ commanded it — "Go!" (Mark 16:15) That is not a suggestion, or a recommendation, but an order. We had better obey, or else miss the greatest joy known to man.

Jesus Christ

JESUS: BURDEN-BEARER NOT BURDEN-GIVER

The servant of God is not a depressor but an up-lifter — He does not condemn but delivers from condemnation. He wears a garment of praise and joy, not of sackcloth. He releases rather than binds and brings light, not gloom and doom. He lifts life's heaviness and does not impose a burden. Our Jesus is the burden-bearer not the burden-giver.

JESUS: THE PRIME EXAMPLE OF INNOCENCE

The death of Jesus exposed the truth about the world, once and for all. It condemned the holy one and the just. It was not just murder by some individual. It wasn't just betrayal by Judas or envy on the part of Caiaphas. The whole system was guilty. Jesus simply did not fit. He was a challenge to Rome, a threat to the established traditions, a challenge to the Temple and institutional religion, a challenge to the authority of the priests and rulers. Here was a man the like of which had never walked on earth before. His love overwhelmed multitudes, His wisdom was matchless, His personal life lived on a level that made the best men feel like clumsy amateurs. He carried absolute authority in His very words. There could be no way to justify killing Him. He was the prime example of innocence. But with such brilliances He could not survive. "Christ died for our sins." (1 Cor 15:3) Thank you, Jesus.

· Godly Gems ·

GUEST OR LORD?

Have you ever seen that little plaque which is on the walls of Christian homes? It says "Christ is the head of this house and the unseen guest for every conversation..." Well we ought to make up our minds what Jesus really is — either a *guest* or the *head*. The head of a house is never a guest. Jesus is our true host, the host of our lives, in all our lives... He is the provider, the welcome, Jesus is never a guest. If you invite Him, He comes as Lord (Rev 3:30). Once He is there things happen though you don't know how they happen. But somehow the bills get paid, and the shortages are supplied, the upsets are settled, the happiness continues, and water turns into wine (Jn 2:6-8).

SPIRIT OF GREATNESS

The woman, who emptied her only wealth upon Christ with a bottle of precious ointment shocked the disciples with such immodest abundance, but it delighted Jesus (Matt 26:6-13). She had captured His very own spirit of greatness. The fragrance filled the house, and as Jesus indicated, it has filled the world ever since. Let's waste ourselves for Jesus. "For He alone is worthy..."

AWE-STRUCK BY THE PERSON OF JESUS

In the gospels people were awe-struck by the person of Jesus whenever they met Him. When that woman of the streets walked in and saw Jesus, she was shocked! She had loved many men, and then she saw Him. The purity, which she felt, that greatness, filled her soul with deep yearnings. She stood and poured out her inexpressible confusion of life in hot tears which, to her horror, fell on His feet, as if she had polluted that sacred person. She hastily tried to dry off those unclean tears and could find nothing with which to do it, except her lavish hair. Never had she had such an experience — she was looking into the eyes of the infinite Son of God. He was all that mattered, He was the peak of life and she had found Him. Her lovers were empty wrecks just as described in the second portion of Jeremiah 2:5, "...they went far from Me and walked after emptiness and became empty." (NASB) Her old life was just as empty — a useless, discarded earthenware pot. Glamor? There was no other glory now, only that of Christ, her Savior. That's Him, Jesus, our blessed Redeemer! "O, what a Savior..."

WE TRUST NO SAVIOR WHO IS DEAD

Jesus crucified and risen from the dead, that is who He is. His wounds and His immortality identify Him. He said "Ye shall know the truth and the truth shall set you free." (Jn 8:32-36) That is the truth we preach — a crucified and risen Lord. We trust no Savior who is dead. *Jesus is alive!*

GOD USED A CRIMINAL TO JUSTIFY HIS SON

When Jesus hung on the cross His disciples deserted Him. But God needed someone to justify His Son. He used one of the criminals crucified with Christ who said "...this man has done nothing wrong." (Lk 23:41) In my opinion this criminal was a man of faith. When he saw Jesus hang on a cross like himself — scourged, mangled, bleeding, and dying — he cried "Lord, remember me, when You come into Your Kingdom" (v. 42). When the Lord was at his lowest point, he believed that this Jesus was the King of a Kingdom and desired to be in it! Jesus replied "...today you will be with me in paradise."(v. 43) What faith! I am sure that no one ever has trusted Jesus under the exact same circumstances. What faith!

JESUS PUT ON OATH

Jesus was put on oath by the High Priest of Israel when He was arrested. On oath He declared, "You will see the Son of Man sitting at the right hand of the Power and coming on the clouds of heaven." (Matt 26:64) He said little else, and this was the most solemn of occasions. He knew His enemies would take hold of this statement and turn it against Him, but He still made it. They judged Him worthy of death for it. But soon afterwards He declared to Pilate that He had come into the world to bear witness to the truth. This is the truth, Jesus will come with power and majesty! If anything is true, this is. The future holds many uncertainties, but they will not matter. Why? Because there is one glorious certainty, which will balance out every fear and distress – Jesus is coming! The stars may fall from heaven, the ordinance of night and day may fail, heaven and earth may pass away, but His Word, His oath, and the promise of His return cannot fail. "For yet a little while, and He who is coming will come and will not tarry." (Heb 10:37) Soon this twilight world will see the dawn, and the glory of the Lord shall cover the earth as the waters cover the sea.

JESUS CHRIST IN COLOR

The Old Testament is an outline of Jesus Christ, but the New Testament photographed Him in color. The Old Testament speaks of God, and Jesus said it spoke of Him. He *fulfilled* the Scriptures — fleshed them out, gave them body and life. Christ is the evidence of what the prophets foretold. He is the Savior of the world.

NO PYROTECHNICS

Christ's great forerunner, John the Baptist, looked for Christ to come with fire and earth-shaking judgment. Jesus sent him a message, "The blind see and the lame walk, the lepers are cleansed and the deaf hear, the dead are raised up and the poor have the gospel preached to them and blessed is he who is not offended because of me." (Lk 7:22) That is God — mercies and kindness, not show-off pyrotechnics. Jesus is the joy of living.

THE RAVE TO THE GRAVE

Sin turns you on and then turns on you. Those who cannot live without drugs and drink cannot live because of them. The rave is the road to the grave. Drugs and alcohol produce only a chemical dream, a mirage in a waterless desert. *Jesus Christ alone is the deliverer!* (Lk 4:18)

RE-POSITIONED

When we begin to believe in the name of Jesus, we are not just "believers," we are re-positioned — it is a personality shift or transfer. We are placed *inside* of what His name represents. The Bible says we have been placed into God's family — this is most impacting. For a sinful person to become a child of God, a miraculous transformation will take place. This is accomplished when we give our lives to Christ.

WHAT JESUS IS...

When they had no shepherd, *Jesus* became the Good Shepherd. When they had no physician, *Jesus* became the great physician. When they had no teacher, *Jesus* became the truth. When the crowds were hungry, *Jesus* became the Bread of Life. In the darkness, they found Jesus to be the Light of the World. Christ's gift to the world was not a new religion, or a new theory about life, or a new formula for heaven. He gave Himself for us, the just for the unjust to bring us to God. Christianity is not a religion — it is Jesus. We can form doctrines around Him, but Jesus did not come to bring us theology. Churches invent rituals and observances, but He never suggested any. Jesus came just to be here, available, never to leave or forsake us personally.

THE IMPOSSIBLE

Jesus Christ told Philip to feed 5000 men in a breadless wilderness. He took fishermen and told them "As you go, heal the sick, raise the dead, cleanse the lepers." (Matt 10:8) Nobody had ever done such things. He charged a paralyzed man, "Take up your bed and walk," (Jn 5:8) to a corpse He cried, "Young man I say to you, Arise," (Lk 7:14) and to an entombed man He commanded, "Lazarus, come forth!" (Jn 11:43) They all did just what He said. Jesus commands the impossible and then makes it possible. He is the same today. That's why we cannot lose.

CHRIST'S PEERLESS AUTHORITY

After the Sermon on the Mount a leper approached the Lord, saying, "If you will, you can make me clean." (Matt 8:2) This perceptive man saw that everything hangs on the will of Jesus. He knew He could, but would He? Faith is not believing that God *can do it*, everybody knows that *He can,* but that He *will do it*. Jesus said, "I will." "I" voiced His peerless authority and *"I will"* His goodness. Nobody else would even touch a leper. Jesus was infinitely different. All Christ said ranked Him alongside the *"I Am"* of the God of Israel. He is Lord. He is willing to touch you now.

BEYOND ANGELS

Christ has elevated those who trust Him to an eternal rank. We shall not only be near Him but like Him. "We are God's children now; it does not yet appear what we shall be, but we know that when he appears we shall be like Him." (1 Jn 3:2) Eternity holds for all who love Jesus, a distinction beyond the angels.

THE PRICE JESUS PAID

People are eternally valuable because Christ sought them in pain, blood, and love. He wants them, even at the cost of the death-rack of the cross. The title deeds of His purchase are in His hands — His wounds. If we were sensitive to such extremities to see and save the lost, would we want anything except what He wants? "Christ's love compels us, because we are convinced that one died for all, and those who live should no longer live for themselves." (2 Cor 5:14-15) By the way, to whom was the precious blood of Jesus paid, the price for our Redemption? To the devil? Oh no, no, no! It was paid into the court of God's justice. We are reconciled with God. "When I see the blood, I will pass over you." (Ex 12:13)

CHRIST IS THE PEAK OF ALL HOPES

Life without Christ is artificial. Drink, drugs, other kinds of *life* are merely a support system, zest from a bottle, gusto from a hypodermic needle. Revelation 3:1 says "You have a reputation of being alive, but you are dead." Only crippled lives need crutches. In contrast, Paul testified he was "as dying, and behold we live." (2 Cor 6:9) Believers have life, I mean *life!* They don't need to rave up what they call a good time, any more than the president needs a rattle. We talk of the good life, bad life, busy life, sad life, empty life, and a fulfilled and happy life. But the Bible introduces a new category, "everlasting life." It is found in Jn 3:36, "Whoever believes in the Son has everlasting life, but whoever rejects the Son will not see life." No higher form of life is thinkable. Jesus Christ is the peak of all hopes.

WE FOUND JESUS

If we follow Jesus' teaching, it leads back to Himself. He is what He taught. He did not present us with a road map to follow for a lifetime ending at God. He said, "He told us to come to Him because He was the way." The Bible has no abstract ideas about God. He appears to us in the living flesh of Christ. Job prayed, "If only I knew where to find Him!" (Job 23:3) Well, we found Him in the resurrected Jesus.

UNIVERSAL LORDSHIP

Jesus covered with His own blood, all the blood that had ever stained the ground. The carpenter of Nazareth made the Life-Gate from the wood of the cross. He outwitted the strategy of Satan, milked the serpent of his venom, out-thought the thinkers, out-fought the fighters, outclassed the mighty, and asserted His universal Lordship. Jesus Christ is Lord.

HOW TO LIVE

The Bible speaks of Christ as being without sin, the spotless Lamb of God. He lived for us the perfect life, leaving us an example to follow in His footsteps. What was His perfection? It was very simple — obedience to God. He did not live by a set of rules to govern every action of His life. He wasn't a walking encyclopedia of the law which He consulted every second from getting up to going to sleep again. He simply did what He knew would please the Father. That is how to live. He lived for us to show us how to live. To please God is all that He wanted. We may have great moral problems, and we don't know which the right thing is to do. Well, there is only one reason why we should be good at all and that is to be like Jesus and to please God. To be like Jesus, all I ask is to be like Him...

GOD CANNOT? HOW DO YOU KNOW?

A medical doctor told me once that God cannot heal a certain eye-disease. I replied, "Before I know what you can do, or cannot do, I have to know everything about you. Your education, your character, your family, your personality, etc... So please tell me how well you know God?" Can God spread a table in the wilderness? (Ps 78:19) Oh yes! *He* is the creator of all things, and us. Almighty, All-powerful, Omniscient, and much more. From Alpha to Omega, which is God's alphabet, the name of *Jesus* includes all letters. Paul says, "I know in whom I have believed..." (2 Tim 1:12), and we, God's children, know as well. We know that we know. Do You? Faith in Him gives us access to the throne of God and His healing bread. You have access!

FOREIGN SHEEP?

Proclaim liberty! Do not preach for effects, for pulpit display, or to charm, excite, or scare people. Do not preach to calm them down. You can preach for all kinds of effects, but Jesus simply announced liberty. (Lk 4:18-19) That day in the synagogue, He proclaimed the start of the Jubilee! He showed them what a true Jubilee would be — deliverance! It would be a Jubilee, not merely for Israel, but for the whole world. A Jubilee for people like the foreigners He mentioned — Naaman, the Syrian leper, and the widow of Zarephath (Lk 4:26-27). The synagogue congregation marveled at this new teaching. They could not imagine the Shepherd of Israel with foreign sheep and were lost in this unfamiliar landscape of Christ's prospects for the entire world. The world He loved was too big for them.

Their fears were roused, murderous passions ignited, and their feelings, which are never far from the surface of man's emotional nexus, were kindled by Jesus' sermon. It sparked an immediate response — the members of the congregation attempted to throw Him over a precipice and kill Him, but He still preached His gospel.

ETERNAL LIFE

God wants us to want eternal *life*, and He wants the sort of people who do want it. He who believes on the Son of God receives everlasting life, which is the blueprint of what He meant us to be. Being joined to Christ Jesus connects us to the fountain and source of all power and being. It does not boost human life but is a new life. Natural experience can be intensified even by religious practices and mind-power programs that stimulate our inner strengths and reserves. But that eternal Life is not a mere stimulant. It is new life, from above. "Our Savior, Jesus Christ, has destroyed death and brought life and immortality to light through the gospel." (2 Tim 1:10) Museums have workshops for cleaning and restoring masterpiece paintings. Great artists would never spend time touching pictures up. They would rather paint a new picture. That is true of Christ. "We are His workmanship." (Eph 2:10) His work in us is not a superficial touch up, an

improvement, "papering over the cracks," as they say. We, read
"In Christ Jesus neither circumcision nor uncircumcision avails
anything, but a new creature." (Gal 6:15) The claim of the gospel
is unique. That is undeniable. It is the "word of life," (Phil 2:16,
1 Jn 1:1) not just an idea, a promise, something to hope for, to seek
or work for. Christ fulfils the promise of God. "The Kingdom of
God is not in word but in power." (1 Cor 4:20) Proclaiming the
word *switches* it on, releasing the power of salvation.

STILL BLESSING

Jesus came blessing people to the very end of His days
on this planet. When the Lord was last seen, "...he had led
them out to the vicinity of Bethany, lifted up his hands and blessed
them. While he was blessing them he left them and was taken up
into heaven." (Lk 24:50-51) His hands were lifted in the gesture of
blessing as clouds drifted over his presence. Then angels assured
the watching disciples, "This same Jesus, who has been taken up
from you into heaven, will come back in the same way you have
seen him go." (Acts 1:11) "In the same way" means with His hands
raised in blessing. Those hands are still raised in blessing, even as I
write these lines. Look at Him.

NOT DEAD, BUT ALIVE

Athaliah, this wicked woman murdered the entire
seed royal, but Joash, one son, was saved as a baby and is
a *type of Christ*. (2 Kings 11:3-16) Jehoiada the priest brought
back Joash and ousted the murderess. She turned up one day to
discover armed men confronting her. Trumpets blew, and the

people rejoiced. The prince "stood by the pillar" whom she had thought had been killed. She was taken and paid for her crimes with her life. Soon a mighty angel will lay hold on the dragon, that old serpent, which is the Devil, and Satan. He will be bound and cast into the bottomless pit and shut up with a seal set upon him, that he should deceive the nations no more. (see Rev 20:1-3) Then we shall see Jesus, the King in His glory "...by the pillar." Trumpets will sound, the people rejoice, the true King will reign in mercy and understanding — the Lamb on the throne. The one the devil tried to destroy at Calvary, the seed royal, the one so many did not know was alive, and many thought did not exist *will be revealed in all His glory.* Jesus Christ, King of kings and Lord of lords.

THE NAME OF JESUS INCLUDES ALL OTHER NAMES

Jesus said, "He that has seen me has seen the Father." (Jn 14:9) If the Father is like Jesus, then God is more wonderful than anyone has ever thought or read. Israel had their wonderful knowledge of God, but Jesus lifted it to the seventh heaven. Speaking about the names of the Lord, such as Yahweh Jireh, the name of Jesus is higher than every other name, because He includes them all. Even the apostles knew this, as evidenced by Scripture. (Acts 4:10-12) Whatever the Yahweh names declared about God, Jesus is. Hebrews 1:3 states He was the "express image" of God's being. One translation says, "the representation of the reality" of God and another says, "the radiance of God's glory." If God is like Jesus, the Almighty is not an unfeeling monolith in a faraway heaven. Jesus is God in action, so is the Holy Spirit. The first Christian martyr, Stephen, is a prime example of God in action. (Acts 7:51-69) When this first Christian martyr lifted his eyes, he saw Jesus standing by the right hand of God, not sitting. (Acts 7:56) The Lord had risen to receive him.

JESUS ALWAYS PAYS

Jesus was Lord of the temple and should not have paid the temple tax, but He paid it for Himself and for Peter anyway. (Matt 17:24-27) Jesus saves, because Jesus pays — He always pays. Whether healing is *in* in the atonement or *through* the atonement, Jesus pays. He is not a King who came to collect tribute, but to bestow His wealth upon us. Christ collected the tax from the mouth of a fish. We are sent as fishers of men, and that is where we shall get our money — by divine provision.

KING IMMORTAL

All anointing-pictures in the Bible point to God's anointed King, our Messiah, or Christ, who would reign forever. People set the years by Israel's kings, but they all died. Our King lives forever and no king will ever succeed Him. We count our years from His reign. It is now the year of our Lord, Anno Domini, 2019. David reigned for forty-years and left the throne to Solomon. But our King has not left His throne to anyone. He is "the King Immortal" (1 Tim 1:17) and said, "I am he that was dead and behold I am alive for ever more." (Rev 1:18)

The
Cross

THE ONLY MAN-MADE THING IN HEAVEN

In Exodus 21:5-6 we read of yet another love law. If a bond servant married a wife, he could not legally take her away with him after he had served his contract with his master. He could keep his wife only if he stayed with his master in permanent servitude. Then, if he agreed, his ear would be pierced with a tool fastening him to the wood of the doorway. The scar would be always there, in the ear and in the door, and it would tell everybody, "I love my wife and have given myself *for* her, so I can give myself *to* her." That is the parable of the love affair of God with humankind. Jesus gave Himself at the cross *for us* so that He could give Himself *to us*. The stab-marks are on His hands and feet for time and eternity — the only man-made thing in heaven. That is what everything is about. God is love. That is why we were born, to be loved and love. To know the love of all loves is the secret of all secrets. Know that, and you possess the answer to the meaning of life. A loveless gospel is a contradiction — a sea without water, the sun without light, honey without sweetness, and bread without substance. The gospel is nothing other than love.

JESUS CARRIED THE CROSS — NOT A PSYCHIATRIST'S COUCH

When Jesus opened the Scriptures to the two disciples who were on their way to Emmaus, He explained, "...what was said in all the Scriptures concerning Himself, saying, 'Did not the Christ have to suffer these things and then enter his glory." (Lk 24:26-27) My concern today is that the same Spirit shall witness to Christ in the same way — to His sufferings, death, and glory. A religion, which consists of psychic experiences, trances, and emotional sensations is not Christianity. Christianity has other aims. Jesus did not come into this world to carry a *psychiatrist's couch, but the cross.* Sinfulness is like leprosy — it kills while dulling the pain. Jesus is first the Savior. Nobody else even claims to be that. Preach Christ and Him crucified, and the Spirit of the ancient Bible-prophets will back you up, penetrating the hearts of all hearers.

WHY OUR WORLD?

We stand back in awe when we read, "God so loved the world" (Jn 3:16) — this world, our world, among a trillion other worlds, where His Son, Jesus, was not sent to be crucified. Our world is not a hobby to Him, not an interesting interlude in eternity watching how free creatures behave. This was the crucial world of eternal issues. Redemption matters would be successfully decided. This is the reason for Calvary. That is why the Holy Spirit is here. God the Father could trust only His Son Jesus Christ and the Holy Spirit to bring it to completion.

WHEN JESUS SAID NOTHING

Things not said can be amazing. In fact, Jesus amazed Pilate, Herod, and the Jewish leaders by saying nothing. He said nothing because He was not afraid. He did not plead for mercy or even for justice. Lying witnesses could not force Him to ask for clemency. He was *the Word.* He would not say what they wanted Him to say, nor wrangle with them. Pilate asked Him if he were a king, but Jesus replied, "You say so." Rome could not intimidate Him. His enemies had this giant figure in their grip, as they thought, but in fact they were no more than puppets dancing on the devil's strings. From the beginning Christ knew His fate was torture, mockery, and the mangling death on the cross, but also a predestined world-changing return from the field of cosmic conflict, having conquered death. *Jesus Christ Is Lord!* Believe it.

PAUL'S DEFENSE WAS A GOOD OFFENSE

Paul defended the gospel by taking the war into the enemy's camp. His defense was a good offense: the offense of the cross. Prison was to him as good a place as any to take the gospel to. It was here that he could do the most damage to the prince of this world, like the imprisoned Samson bringing the house down on his foes. Paul was not concerned with motivation or circumstance. There was a far more important consideration, "...that in every way, whether from false motives or true, Christ is preached. And because of this I rejoice." (Phil 1:18) And he encouraged other believers to adopt this position, "...without being frightened in any way by those who oppose you" (v. 28).

CRUCIFIXION

The story of Jesus doesn't end with a crucifixion, if it did, the cross would be a symbol of crushing defeat and despair. The good news is that Jesus not only destroyed the power of sin on the cross, He also destroyed the power of death. On the third day, He was raised back to life, triumphant over darkness, death, and the Devil. *Jesus is alive!*

JESUS IS THE JESUS OF THE BIBLE

The apostles preached Christ and Him crucified. Nothing could have been more calculated to ensure the failure of their mission. Crucifixion was for the worst criminals, the lowest of the low. Put a man on a cross and everybody mocked him. In no way was a crucified Jesus the ideal figure to appeal to either Jews or Gentiles. "He was despised and rejected." (Is 53:3) But that is the Jesus they knew and that is the only Jesus they preached. And by their preaching they conquered the world. People must adjust to what God is. We don't preach a god made in their image. We must preach the Jesus of the gospels and not some popular ideal but the Jesus of Calvary. If we preach Him as no more than a healer and a sweet, gentle, kind Jesus, then we have concealed the truth. We cannot allow our message to be influenced by public consensus, human notions, or prejudice. People who won't face facts will learn the hard way. Jesus is the Jesus of the Bible. We can't reshape Him according to the ideals of the world.

HUMILITY OF CHRIST

Although Jesus was spat upon, insulted, scourged, and crucified by man, He was never humiliated, because Philippians 2:8 says, "He humbled Himself." He voluntarily took the lowest place, and nobody could push Him lower. O, what a Savior!

CALVARY — GOD'S GLORY

Like the sun is light, God is glory, but living glory. Whatever He touches is glorified. He made even the vandalized tree glorious when they nailed Him to it. The cross shines as our beacon in the godless night of this world. When Moses saw God's glory, his own face shone. When God comes, He comes in glory and fills us with glory, as well as our homes and future. No Christian home should be dull and lifeless, but bursting with vitality, activity, joy, and richness.

TO WHERE DID OUR SIN GO?

What really happened to our sin, where did it go? When we sin, it seems it is only a little trickle, but there are many trickles. They run together and became a brook, a stream, a river, an Amazon flowing to somewhere. That drain, that somewhere was Calvary, or rather God in Christ at Calvary. "For God was in Christ, reconciling the world to himself, no longer counting people's sins against them." (2 Cor 5:19) That is about all we can say. His suffering in His redeeming work is unutterable and incomprehensible. Only God can appreciate what God experiences. Just stop and think about it. "O come, let us adore Him, Christ the Lord."

BREAD AND WINE IN REMEMBRANCE

And if anything should be remembered about Jesus it is represented here with bread and wine. It is not some doctrine or theory about God, some metaphysic, it is a piece of hard history, factual, concrete, palpable. This bread is words turned into substance, words in a material which form truth that is edible, a fact that is drinkable. We have not come here to think about an abstract metaphysic, something mystical and remote. We are remembering history, what Jesus did for us — He walked into the furnace of judgment, of physical pain, horror, and hell for you and for me. That's not religion, but an event with infinite significance.

CALVARY SCARS

There are new gods today, but where are their Calvary scars? Christ stands near us, so obvious. "Behold I stand at the door and knock!" (Rev 3:20) It is when we see His wounded hands and side, that we cry, "My Lord and my God." The true God has always shared our sorrows, carried our grief, and borne our sins, drinking the deepest cup of anguish, accepting the tragedy of mankind within Himself. He was numbered with the transgressors, standing in solidarity with the guilty and identifies with us all. "In all their afflictions He was afflicted."

OPPOSING FORCES

Hanging on the cross, Jesus appeared to be anything but powerful. Mocked by the crowds, tortured by the soldiers, deserted by His friends, slowly bleeding to death, Jesus was utterly helpless. Yet it was from this cross of weakness that God released His awesome power. How can this be? One way to picture it is through nuclear physics. In every atom, positive and negative forces hold together in balance. But when the atom splits, positive divides from negative, unleashing great force either for destruction or benefit.

Something like this happened on the cross. As He hung there, Jesus experienced two opposing forces in Himself — the negative of our sins and the positive of God's love. Though Jesus was the holy, perfect Son of God, He was made "sin for us" on the cross. There He became the cosmic center where all evil and goodness converged. Finally, like a splitting atom, the negative forces dispersed when Jesus overcame evil, releasing new powers of righteousness and resurrection. Within three days this new power exploded like a nuclear blast when Christ gloriously and triumphantly rose from the dead. Evil, death, guilt, and fear were conquered, while the saving power of God's love was released for everyone who asks for it.

THE CROSS-LOGO

The cross is the symbol or logo of the Christian faith. It belongs to Jesus alone. No founder or leader of another religion would dare to use this logo because it stands for something that they themselves have never done! None of them have been crucified for the sins of the world. None of them have been raised from the dead. None of them can give us the help we so desperately need. Only Jesus can save us. As He said: "I am the way, the truth, and the life; no one goes to the Father except by me." (Jn 14:6) No matter where you look: there is no other Savior from sin.

ETERNAL PURPOSES

"In the beginning God..." (Gen 1:1) God is there in every true beginning! We do not begin at all until we come to Him — we are simply going nowhere and doing nothing, like people on a treadmill. The Greeks thought that time went in circles, the same things happening repeatedly. But this astonishing book, the Bible, cuts right across heathen guesses at how things function. God's ways are eternal, not repetitive. When our lives are tied in with His, we are carried along in His purposes as He sweeps from the eternal past to the eternal future, the eternal *Alpha* and *Omega*, *Jesus Christ*. Entrust your life to Him.

NO CROSS-PURPOSES WITH CHRIST

Anyone who lives at cross-purposes with Christ's cross gets eventually blown away like an insect in a hurricane. There is safety and fulfilment only in following Jesus.

RE-ARRANGED

At the cross Jesus rearranged the letters of EVIL to LIVE. "Look and live, my brother, live, look to Jesus now and live[2]..."

DROP BY DROP

Long ago, drop by drop, the gold of Christ's life-blood ebbed out of His heart. It stained Calvary's hill, spelling out in crimson letters the story of the love that surpasses all love. Today, hundreds of millions around the whole world — the simple and the wise, those who live in jungles and those who live in concrete apartment blocks, factory workers and academics — take that message as the truth above all truths. It shows us the concerns of God's heart and a wisdom which soars far above our cloud-hopping minds. Great intellects have bowed to it. Saul of Tarsus, once full of biting hatred, came to see the cross as the logic of God. He said it was a stumbling block to Jews and foolishness to Greeks but the power of God to all that believe (1 Cor 1:23-24). Do you believe?

IMAGE OF GOD IN MAN

Tempted by the Pharisees whether people were to pay taxes, Jesus asked for a coin and said, "Whose image and inscription is on it?" They replied "Caesar's." The Lord answered, "Give to Caesar what is Caesar's and to God what is God's." (Lk 20:21-25) That was a hammer! The money belonged to Caesar because it bore Caesar's image. But man should belong to God, because we are created in God's image. God has a righteous claim on all of us. We were stamped with His image when He made us. Satan tries to deface God's image in us with *sin* — he wants to replace it with his own. But God stepped in and our Creator became our Redeemer. Jesus bought us back by redeeming us by His blood. His precious blood was the currency, the means of payment. That is the reason for Christ's death on the cross. Jesus says, "My son, give me your heart." (Prov 23:26) Simple? Oh yes, but not simplistic! It is profound!

LEGAL IMMIGRANT

The Kingdom of God was established through a titanic battle and the victory of Christ. His blood marks its foundations. Calvary is the source of the redemptive dynamic of God, the nuclear power-drive of the gospel, and of all the gifts of the Spirit. For those moving into a real Holy Spirit-relationship, we are obliged to mention that modern religionists are busy building Calvary bypasses. Roads that avoid Calvary prove to go nowhere. There are no indirect routes. The Kingdom of God has a check-point and border control, and it is at the Cross. Without having been to Calvary, everybody lives a second-class existence as illegal immigrant. Passport and entry permits are repentance and faith in Christ Jesus. Then we may enter the Kingdom with the full privileges of citizens, "...no longer strangers and foreigners, but fellow citizens with the saints and members of the household of God." (Eph 2:19) The "covenants of promise" are ours.

ROADBLOCK

Jesus spoke about the broad way to hell "that leads to destruction," jam-packed with people. (Matt 7:13) He then planted His cross in the middle of that highway, spreading out His arms. It turned into the biggest roadblock of all times. "Repent" is the message — which means, change your direction. Those who do repent and believe turn around and move in the opposite direction — heavenward! *Jesus saves!*

NO EXTINCT VOLCANO

Calvary is not an extinct volcano. Eternal fires are there for all who spiritually visit that place. Those shuddering hours of crucifixion were a special work but not a special peak. His love has neither peaks nor valleys, waves or troughs. His compassions are steadfast and "new every morning." (Lam 3:23) The cross was not a desperate, frustrated, spur-of-the-moment attempt to reach us. It was part of the original plan — Christ's journey to Jerusalem and the cross began before the foundation of the world. But it was not the end. "Then the disciples went out and preached everywhere, and the Lord worked with them." (Mk 16:20) And He has never stopped going with them.

MATCHLESS TRUTH

There is no religion or message in the entire world like the gospel. No religion in the world has a cross and a savior bearing the sins of the whole world. The cross is the great, profound, magnificent, unconquerable, unchangeable, and matchless truth. It towers above all mere religious ideas. (Acts 13:38)

RISKING EVERYTHING

When Jesus healed the sick it was not just sheer voltage power He wielded, but the power of His conquering love. He healed the sick by His stripes — that was the secret wonder of His anointing. He healed a withered arm, although it provoked men to plot against His life. He risked everything, and would go to any length, even the Cross, for the sake of the suffering. Pain and the ministry of healing are strangely linked. When some of us are willing to know, "the fellowship of His sufferings," and feel the same anointing of love, as Jesus had... When there are those who embrace the same heartbreaking pity that forgets self, and that will make any sacrifice for the afflicted, as Jesus did — identifying with the sufferer in such a way that we would share suffering to ease others' pain, as Jesus did, and become "touched with the feeling of their infirmity" and "afflicted in all their affliction," as Jesus was... Then perhaps fewer people would go home unhealed.

FULLEST GLORY IN JESUS CHRIST

The revelation of God comes in its fullest glory in Jesus Christ, which is why we preach Him (see Jn 1:18). It is He who interprets the God of the Old Testament. His astoundingly wonderful life reveals an astoundingly wonderful God. We see Him most truly as He is for us when He hangs on the cross. If we forget that, we know nothing about God. Anything beyond that is of no lasting value.

LEAVING THE MEDICINE IN THE BOTTLE

Sick people who do not read the Bible leave the medicine in the bottle tightly corked. Those without faith should be warned that if they open the Bible, they are likely to finish up as believers. The Bible brings us to the cross. Real faith does not start at the university. We will have less if we go there without any! If we have not been to where Christ saves not even a Doctor of Theology will do.

THE CROSS IS NO FICTION

True forgiveness is as substantial as the cross on which Christ bought it. It rests on a rock-solid foundation, on the historic fact of Jesus Christ's redemptive sacrifice (1 Pet 3:18). The cross was no fiction. Real blood fell on real ground, and this real blood brings real cleansing to real sinners and does much more besides.

PERSECUTION

Paul the apostle appeared in court. He lifted his hands, fetters clanking, and preached Christ to the proud and noble assembly in their splendor of purple and gold. They were destined to be remembered but only because Paul stood before them that day. Their prisoner immortalized them — a little Roman Jew from Tarsus. While he spoke, he was changing the future of Europe and the whole world. Smelling of jail, Paul's great heart was breaking in pity for them, kings, companions, courtiers, and all. He added his defense saying, "I pray God that not only you but all who are listening to me today may become what I am, except for these chains." (Acts 26:29) He knew... Only the saved do know. Only the born-again.

TWO CROSSES

There are two crosses, Christ's and ours (Matt 16:24). His cross saves us eternally. Our cross saves us from wasting our lives. A Christ-less life is a wasted life. If we have life by the Holy Spirit, let us also walk by the Spirit.

Salvation

GOD BOTHERS WITH US

Job asked why God bothered with him in his sin. (Job 3:20-23) MSG God fully answered that question at the cross of Calvary, where the curtains are drawn aside to show what sin has been doing. God still bothers people with His salvation today, because this day is the day of salvation. "My son give me your heart and let your eyes delight in my ways." (Prov 23:26) Well, do it today.

GOD FIXES OUR VALUE

The cross was salvation's cost to God and fixes its value to us. Salvation must be measured by the massive effort behind it, namely the life, death, and resurrection of Jesus, the Son of God. We are entitled to expect a tremendous outcome for that outlay. The Calvary-event tore heaven open, darkened the sun, and made Jesus Christ sweat blood bringing angels to help Him. Why all that? Nothing, but nothing could justify it except world redemption, and the guarantee of salvation for every individual who put their trust in Jesus.

THE GAP OF FAITH CAN BE LEAPED AS FAST AS LIGHT

The woman of Samaria is a powerful lesson from history on faith (see John, Chapter 4). It illustrates the fact that a sinner can take a profound leap of faith into the heights of the supernatural. She was a nameless woman that came to draw water from a well. Jesus asked her for a drink from the well and astonished her, because He offered her "living water." The lady decided to humor Him, thinking Him slightly irrational. So, she just said, "You just give me a drink like that, so I won't get thirsty and keep coming back to this well!" The woman certainly expected nothing of the kind. Jesus simply said, "Go and bring your husband." She put on an air of innocence and said she had no husband. Jesus then shattered her with her sullied life and record of husbands. She stared at Him shocked, and said, "I can see you are a prophet." She had advanced in perception and faith. Jesus next shook her ideas about worship. Christ's reply was totally new... Worship had nothing to do with place or time. Worship was anywhere, everywhere, and always. She now felt lost in such a theological depth, so she tried to edge around it saying that such matters would be settled when the Messiah came. The woman was getting closer, and then Jesus said, "I who speak to you am He." Her faith soared. Excited, she rushed into the town telling everybody about Jesus and asking, "Could this be the Messiah?" The woman had believed, sinful as she was. In this incident, the development of faith is swift and always ends by a commitment, a relationship, and a taking hold of Jesus personally. Being a mere believer in God has a long way to go, but it is a gap that can be leaped, as fast as light. One second far from God and the next second bound to Him eternally through faith — "one with Christ." We become in a moment, as Jesus said about the disciples to the Father, "They are Yours . . . and Yours are Mine, and I am glorified in them . . . and none of them are lost." (Jn 17:9-12)

"MADE AT CALVARY"

Salvation was not produced in the New Jerusalem, a package deal imported from above, dropped from the blue skies. Salvation came by an act of God on earth, at Calvary. People saw it happening: the bleeding Savior Jesus Christ bearing our sin. Mercy was opened and from its historical beginnings it reaches eternity. It is a gospel to be announced, accepted, and enjoyed — earthly reality with superior effect.

SWEPT WITH THE PRAISE OF JESUS

Jesus Christ was a ransom and a price was paid — that's the Bible. But salvation was not a simple cash down transaction, or a commercial agreement. There was a cost to salvation. The Good Friday scenes at Calvary make that obvious enough. But did we see it all? How heavy really was that cost? What precisely did it exact of our Lord? Perhaps an indication of His sacrifice is given us in the Book of Revelation. It describes the whole universe being swept with His praise. Every creature in heaven and earth knows that none of them is worthy, only Jesus. He had penetrated a far land of darkness where nobody else had trod. They multiply accolades and exhaust language to match the just reward of His unparalleled work. The cause of such worthiness was observable only in a measure even by those who watched Him in His dying hours. But it was not the total cost. We must consider another tremendous fact, that Christ was one with the Father. Infinity shared with the sin-bearer. The black hurricanes surging around the hill at Jerusalem swept also around the throne above. Christ accepted our judgement but, "God was in Christ reconciling the world unto Himself." (2 Cor 5:19) The vastness of the heart of God found a place for the sorrows of mankind. The music of heaven transcended to a major key.

THE CROSS — THE CONVERGING POINT

*D*riving on major road systems we see warnings, "Roads Merge." Within a quarter of a mile or so, we find ourselves moving along with traffic from some other road. That is what happens at the cross of Calvary — it is the converging point. There we move along with the traffic of God into harmony with His will. Take a wrong turn, miss the cross, and we miss the direction in which everything is moving. The meaning and intention for which the Lord God made everything would be lost. We drive on into ever deepening shadows. I can't speculate about how that can be, but I take it as I read it in the Bible. Somehow the sacrifice of Jesus is built into the foundation of the world. The cross is there and always has been. I stand before this world of ours and see it in a different light than even our best science can discover. The wonder of life springs from God's eternal love, and that wonder is especially seen in salvation. The world does not exist for itself, but for the heirs of salvation. We touch the Rock there — the Rock on which everything is built.

GOD'S ARMOR

*T*he world has its armor, like Goliath of Gath, its helmet of education, its spear of science, its sword of reason, its shield of cold indifference. But God has His anointed "Davids" today, not one but millions! We have the whole armor of God, the helmet of salvation, the shield of faith, the sword of the Word of God, and our feet are shod with the footwear of peace. We need not be afraid — the battle is the Lord's and ours the victory.

JESUS SAVES

The words, "Jesus saves," embrace everything that defeats us. Every life has a thousand needs. Salvation touches all weaknesses, reaching into the past and future — it is for body, soul, and mind, for earth and for heaven. Jesus saves us from our sins... From folly, failure, and fear, from pride and illusion, from the devil's deceit and every threatening circumstance. Christ is the Master of It all. Yes, Jesus saves!

A SUPREME ACT WITH A SUPREME OUTCOME

The cross seemed to sum up all the negative forces that depress humanity. But this was no defeat, it was omnipotence in action — omnipotence turning every negative into a positive, a supreme act with a supreme outcome. Christ wept for the weeping; He became helpless for the helpless, unwanted for the unwanted, and unclean for the unclean; He faced death for the dying, and horror for the terrified. He suffered injustice for all who were oppressed, and He surrendered his reputation for all the nonentities in the world. Beyond all miracles, Christ's death on the cross at Calvary was an act of such greatness that the world will never be able to get over it. What an amazing outcome.

COMPULSIONS UNHINGED

Compulsions unhinge a healthy person. He either burns up with fever or cannot keep warm. He is dominated by a single appetite or longing, which becomes stronger than reason or conscience. He is an addict. On the other hand, holiness is simply spiritual health and brings peace. Nobody can enjoy the world except he who enjoys God. Self-control arises from wholeness at that moment when Jesus says, "Go in peace, your faith had made you whole." (Mk 5:34)

LOVE IS THE GENIUS OF GOD

Love is the genius of God. The fruit of the Spirit, Love, is a passion for service and holiness. What the unsaved regard as sacrifice is an outlet of joy to the Christian. Love has its own imperatives and must take up the cross! God's own utter loss of His Son is difficult to justify, but God justifies His "unspeakable gift" to us by His own character. Love must give. Jesus came to fulfill the law and bound Himself forever to us. He took upon Himself the form of a man, of a servant — and was pierced (Ps 40:6). The Christian does not stagger along with two tablets of stone. He is a person shining with the love of God.

CASTING A SHAFT OF LIGHT

It is said that "coming events cast their shadows before them," but *the coming of Jesus Christ* cast a shaft of light before it. It is almost as if God was so full of it, that He couldn't keep quiet about it. Someone was coming! It is hard to keep a secret like this. Even before Adam was expelled from Eden God let it out. He made a mysterious remark that Eve's offspring would crush the head of the serpent (Gen 3:15). It happened at last, the crowning event, "God so loved the world that He gave His only begotten Son," (John 3:16) and "In the fullness of time, God sent forth His Son," (Gal 4:4) yet again, "The Word was made flesh and dwelt among us." (Jn 1:14) People who knew Him were full of Him. Jesus had to come. Without Him nothing was complete, and we were not. "For thou hast created all things, and for thy pleasure they are and were created." (Rev 4:11) KJV

EXPLAIN JESUS

If people don't believe — explain Jesus! If death is the end — explain Jesus! If life is meaningless — explain Jesus! If this world is the whole show — explain Jesus! If evil is permanent — explain Jesus! The cross is an objective force against evil. The love of God is streaming like a river of goodness. To get in, means to be carried on the swelling waves of eternal life.

THE RED-LINE

The cross of Christ is the biggest roadblock on the highway to hell. It is the final red line which dare not be ignored. A friend of mine told me of a notice he saw on the Alps in Switzerland, saying "It is dangerous to step over the fence." It was the most sublime understatement, for there was nothing on the other side of the fence to step on to whatsoever except thin air and the rocks two thousand feet below. Do not consider climbing over the fence of God's salvation. As the Swiss put it, "It is dangerous!" But the good news is that Christ saves in such situations. You will be forever, "...safe in the arms of Jesus." Trust Him.

MILITANT MERCY

The gospel does not threaten sinners. It is glad news, not mad news. Yet Jesus talked more about hell than heaven — not as a *threat* but as a *warning*. There is something I'd call *militant mercy*. When a fast-moving car approaches a child, we would snatch it from danger. It may be rough, but it is true mercy. That's what Jesus does! *He saves!*

CAT AT THE DOOR

Sin is like a cat at the door, it slips in before you know it. *(Matt 24:42)*

HOW SALVATION WORKS

Christ died *for* our sins so that we will not die *in* our sins (Jn 8:21). Once washed in the blood of Jesus, we are no longer *in sin*, but *in Christ*. We shall "not come into judgment" because Jesus was judged for us when dying on the cross (Jn 5:24). This is how salvation works and only *Jesus* makes it possible.

YOU MUST...

When Jesus said, "You must be born again," it meant that He also had to say almost immediately, "The Son of Man must be lifted up." (Jn 3:7 and 14) He used the same word, "*must.*" Our need becomes His need to meet our need.

GOD RUNNING TO MEET A SINNER

God running to meet a sinner! "And he arose..." (Lk 15:20). Having waited daily, his father saw him from afar. The son staggered home, but the old father *ran.* For every step you take toward Jesus, Jesus takes ten steps towards you, because He loves you! Why did the father run? He was worried his son might still change his mind and return to the pigsty. God running to meet a sinner.

NOTHING IS TOO EXTRAVAGANT

Those who met Jesus were infected with his "bigness" syndrome. Zacchaeus spent an hour with Jesus and his rocky heart splintered into shards of excessive generosity. Perhaps some today might have cautioned him about letting enthusiasm run away with him, but Jesus did not. A woman poured perfume on His feet (Lk 7:38) and He defended her. In Bethany another woman emptied the total contents of an alabaster jar of very expensive perfume on His head (Matt 26:6). It was her most saleable asset, her nest egg, but she did not think it was too much to give. Nothing is too extravagant where love, or God are involved. That woman kept nothing in reserve, just like the widow whom Jesus watched putting her whole livelihood into the offering. Perhaps some are secretly puzzled that Jesus praised these excessive acts but His way of life overflows and floods the narrows and shallows of self-centered existence. Jesus wants the world to be filled with whole-hearted folk, servers and givers who do not think of the cost. Shall we be part of it?

IN OPPOSITE DIRECTIONS

A big crowd is following Jesus as He approaches the town of Nain (Lk 7:11-17). Then He met another big crowd going in the opposite direction. The Nain crowd had death at its head, the corpse of a young man, and the whole town had turned out distressed for the mother, a widow, weeping and demonstrating as only easterners can. But the crowd with Jesus had Him, the Resurrection and the Life, at its head and it was jubilant. This was a group of excited folks. Hundreds of them had been at death's door, sick, deaf, blind, or crippled, and now they were healthy, the deaf hearing, the blind seeing, and the cripples dancing — all gladly following for miles to Nain. The two crowds stand for two streams of humanity, which are still moving along today — in opposite directions! One has no future but the grave, and the other is led by Christ who said, "Whoever believes in me will never die." (Jn 11:26) And Jesus beckons us to join His train today, rejoicing in Him — just in Him!

TOWERING SALVATION JESUS SAVES.

And what a salvation! It tore heaven open and sent the Son of God battering hell and all its works! Divine involvement for us and our salvation, has exhausted descriptive genius. Pictures, sculptures, poems, hymns, books, music, and still Christ's salvation towers over all the works of men which it inspires.

A NEW RACE

Christians are a new race. They mystified the pagans. They knew what was never known on earth before. The Lord's resurrection had taken place. Christ was risen from the pit of death, made mockery of the silly seal of Rome upon His tomb. But Jesus broke something far mightier than a waxen seal of the then world-power. He broke the power of death, "O death where is your victory?" (1 Cor 15:55)

THE CONQUEROR WITH
THE BLEEDING FEET

The crowds had more than once wanted Jesus to be king, and to conquer the much-hated Roman army of occupation. But He refused. His servants did not fight to make Him an earthly lord. He had a new way. Jesus conquered this Roman captain who oversaw the squad of soldiers that carried out the crucifixion. Nailed and helpless, yet Christ conquered this military commander. Within 300 years, Rome itself had been conquered.

Not by the jackbooted feet of military forces, but by the bleeding feet of this man hanging there. O praise the Lord! The last pagan emperor, named Julian, tried to restore the old worship of the gods, but the tides released by Christ's death and resurrection were too powerful. Julian cried out in agony, "O Galilean, you have conquered!"

LOVE — WORKS

Jesus came to "...work the works of God" and all His works are love works. God is love. You can't stop the sun from shining and you can't stop God from loving. The sun is for shining and God is for loving. That is why Jesus came. "God so loved the world that He gave His only begotten Son." That purpose was worked out in all Christ did. God had many purposes, and what He does has many an outcome, but He has only one motive.... LOVE!

WE ARE ALL SPECIAL TO JESUS

Jesus said, "I do always those things that please the Father." (Jn 8:29) What had He seen the Father do? He had seen Him stoop over the wretched tribes in Egypt, pick them up and make them great. Jesus did the same. He chose fishermen, not princes, to be His ambassadors. The gospels show Him, again and again, meeting the unwanted and giving them a place. His outreach to the discarded is a moving part of the gospel story. Jesus is with the "lost" and the "last." The lost He finds, and to the last he says, "The last shall be first." (Matt 20:16) In Christ, everyone is someone, even the guilty thief on the cross. Christ never treated people as "the masses." To Him, we are all individuals, all special, and all loved.

POLITICS

When a ruler of Israel came to Jesus for help Jesus did not give him any political advice. Christ was not a divine "spin doctor," a counsellor of rulers. He said something that puzzled the man. "You must be born again." (Jn 3:3) A man is born-again when he rests his confidence in Christ — it is a transforming moment. The world and life look different when we have come to Christ, to trust in Christ *and be born again*. That is the way to be good and great. He said some are born great, but not many are, but we can be born-again great. Jesus was saying that Israel needed a spiritual revolution not a political revolution. Political revolutions sometimes are very necessary, but they still put human beings into power that are fallible and imperfect. Great people are needed, but greatness comes from goodness and goodness comes from Jesus Christ. He never lets people down or nations that trust Him. Some people run on clever sayings and philosophies, but we can't remember them all, especially when under stress. A man needs only one walking stick. A dozen sticks are a burden, not a help. The Bible tells us what the great principle of life is, "The fear of the Lord is the beginning of wisdom." (Prov 9:10) That fear is the loving fear for a father. Fear God and love God and everything falls into place. Let us pray for our politicians.

THE CROSS CANNOT BE REMOVED FROM HISTORY

God is a Rock and He is the Rock of our salvation, the Rock that never rocks (Ps 95). Our salvation is an immovable, imperishable rock. It no longer relies even upon the promise of God, firm as His Word is. We have moved from Scriptures of promise to the Christian age of fulfillment. The work is accomplished and what is done can never be undone. The cross can never be written out of history.

UNALTERABLE TRUTH

The cross is a declaration to mankind, and it is God's answer to our world — real, historic, concrete, and right up to date. "Where is the disputer of this age?" (1 Cor 1:20) Nobody can rewrite history to ensure that the crucifixion did not take place. The rocky crag of Calvary represents the rock of eternal and unalterable truth.

A WOUNDED CHRIST

The blood of Jesus speaks the truth about God. Christian truth is not a delicate blossom cultivated like a lily in a hot house. God did not deal with sin from a cushioned pulpit but nailed it to a cruel Roman cross. Only a wounded Christ can come to a wounded world. Our kind of world needs that kind of Savior.

COLOSSAL TRIUMPH

Either the cross was the most colossal blunder, a tragic demonstration of the uselessness of being a good man, or else it was the world's most colossal triumph. It was in fact the decisive victory for world's redemption. A Roman spear opened Christ's side and exposed the very heart of God — all love. That's the price. That price! For what? To set preachers up in business? For a few "religious freaks"? A mountain in birth pangs bringing forth a mouse? Was that mount Calvary — lighting only a church candle? Or did it bring in the dawn?

YES, TO THE WILL OF GOD

When Jesus came to Jerusalem to save it, He said He could do nothing to save them. "O Jerusalem, Jerusalem ... how often I have longed to gather your children together ... but you were not willing. Look, your house is left to you desolate." (Mt 23:37-38, Lk 13:34-35) (He said literally, "I willed — but you willed not"). Whether Jew or Greek or anybody else, we *must* make our decision! Jerusalem rejected its only Savior and was totally and mercilessly destroyed shortly after that. It is as serious as that. Nobody is kidnapped to heaven. There are only the redeemed. God wills to save you now, and now you must will that you want to be saved before it is too late. I feel the Holy Spirit urges me to write this. Say *yes* to the will of God.

MORTALLY WOUNDED

Jesus came into the world not to defend heaven but as a conquering man of war "to destroy the works of the devil."(1 Jn 3:8) Christ took the battle into the enemy's camp, invaded hell, relentlessly flushed out the foe, hunted him down, drove Satan into a corner, gave him neither quarter nor mercy, bruised that serpent's head and left him defeated and useless. Satan is not "alive and well on planet earth." Jesus has mortally wounded him. Christ's victory is ours. Rejoice.

THE CARPENTER OF NAZARETH

Jesus, the carpenter of Nazareth, turned the wood of the cross into the door to life. That is the deep heart of the good news — the cross has the power to transform us. Minus is turned to plus and negative to positive. On the cross, darkness changes to light, death to life, hate to love, chains to freedom, fear to faith, despair to joy, brokenness to wholeness, hell to heaven...

PRECIOUS BLOOD

Blood has a very short life span. Over half of it is liquid, called plasma, and most of the rest of it is made up of red cells, which die after 120 days and are constantly being replaced. In contrast, the most durable thing on earth is probably gold. Not even salt water affects it — even if it lies in it for centuries. These facts make a comment by Peter, the leading Christian apostle, seem very strange, "It was not with perishable things such as silver or gold that you were redeemed... but with the precious blood of Christ, a lamb without blemish or defect." (1 Pet 1:18-19) Gold is not perishable whereas blood certainly is. But Peter knew what he was talking about and meant to startle us into seeing a tremendous truth. The world thinks money is everything, but Peter intended us to see that it has no spiritual value whatever. There are no spiritual cash payment bargains. In real terms, only the blood of Jesus has lasting value. When heaven and earth vanish, the redeeming power of Christ's blood will continue, it shall never lose its power.

REJECTS BECOME GOD'S ELECTS

The Bible has a roll call of failures that became a force in the world. Moses and Paul had been murderers, Noah and Lot got drunk, Joseph a long-term jail bird, Peter who denied Jesus, Gideon who was scared, and the rest of God's recycled heroes... But something happened. The Lord crossed their paths and the world's rejects became God's elects. He's knocking on our door today.

UNDER THE TABLECLOTH

Suppose you have a table with a big stain on its surface. When visitors come, you cover the stain with a tablecloth so that nobody will notice it. Then the stain is covered, but not removed. This is the meaning of the Old Testament word "atonement" — covered. The rivers of blood of the millions of sacrificial animals were not able to "take away" sin, but only to cover it for a while. That is the reason why John the Baptist was so excited and cried out, "Look, the Lamb of God, who takes away the sin of the world," when he saw Jesus come to the river Jordan (Jn 1:29). Jesus' blood works under the "tablecloth" and behind every facade and make-up. It tackles the root-sins and problems of all people who put their faith in Jesus Christ. The blood of the Lamb of God alone has value and power to save. His sacrifice was sufficient for all men, women, boys, and girls, for all ages.

BORN AGAIN

Christ's hell-shattering work has opened heaven's fountain of resources for all struggling souls. "He that believes in Me, has life." Being saved means being "born again." "To as many as received Him, to them gave He power to become the sons of God." (Jn 1:12) Getting it right meant the status of a prince of heaven, "passing from death to life," being "a new creature in Christ Jesus," like a beautiful winged creature emerges from a cocoon.

GRAND SCALE

God did not come down to give us some of His wisdom, or rules, or teach us ideals. He came as fire, not thought, philosophy, or theory — but burning, passionate, active intervention in human affairs to set people free, and on a scale undreamed of. The slaves in Egypt never asked or imagined of what He would do. God meant the world to know what He was. He did not release them quietly, creeping past the guards, or hurrying them breathlessly from cover to cover cunningly like shadows in the night. He did it flamboyantly, in a way nobody could ever forget. The God of the burning bush did it on the grand scale, challenging the most powerful man on earth, Pharaoh, King of Egypt, with his cohorts, chariots, spearmen, and mighty swordsmen — ending with a triumph such as never since has been repeated, right under the royal nose of the monarch. We serve a mighty God.

WHAT WE COST GOD

We are worth nothing except what we cost God. People are seeking truth, and here it is — "...the Son of God loved us and gave Himself for us." (Eph 5:2) That love is not a theory but a fact of history. It is the ultimate truth the philosophers seek — love is beyond reason. "And the peace of God, which surpasses all understanding..." (Phil 4:7) ...and not-understanding. God's heart made His mind up. His love story has a happy ending that never ends.

NO CHURCH SAVES

No church can save us. This is because no church, neither mine nor yours, died for us. No pope, no bishop, no pastor, no evangelist can save us, because none of them died for us. But here is the name of the one who did die for us. It is *Jesus! Jesus! Jesus! Jesus saves.*

WHERE ARE YOU?

God called, "Adam, where are you?" meaning, if you think you can be without me, I cannot be without you.

"Adam, where are you?" God is calling you. Give Him your position and He will change your situation.

DAY OF SALVATION

The gospel is all miracle. Miracle power lies within it and miracle power enables those who preach it. Miracles of providence will assist its propagation. It has not dawned yet upon some that this is *the day of salvation* as never in all history. With unprecedented advances on all fronts, and more people being saved, healed, and filled with the Holy Spirit than ever before, more churches are being opened daily than at any time in the last 2000 years. The prophecies are being fulfilled, and soon, the roll will be called.

LIKE BREATHING

The gospel is like breathing — there's no future in the alternative. We may have the right of choice, but options here are strictly limited. Without breathing we physically die and without believing in Jesus we are eternally lost. Similarly, God's Word is the only cure for sin known to us, to save and bless, alternatives won't do better here than a good game of chess. They are no answer to the crippling power of sin and do not free from guilt. People desperately need salvation and only Jesus saves, with His blood spilt.

NOT A HUMAN AMENDMENT

The gospel is not an amendment to improve some human resolve. It declares all debates illegal to find other means of salvation. No matter how humble the gospel preacher; he is the Lord's appointed teacher. He speaks with His authority, with original clarity, and fearless bravery. The gospel is not a proposition for discussion, but truth that set's us free, declaring an amnesty for all sinners, which is Good News — for you and me.

JESUS: PROPHECY FULFILLED

Names are spiritually important in the Bible: The name of *Jesus* was given, according to Matthew 1:21b to fulfill prophecy, to give Him human identity; to link man with God, to represent salvation as the work of God, to signify new spiritual understanding; and because, "He shall save His people from their sins." Some names were prophecies. Isaiah used whole sentences for his children. One was, "Maher shalal hash baz" (Isaiah 8:1), meaning, "Speed the spoil. Hasten the prey." But the name of Jesus was not a prophecy. It was a fulfillment of prophecy. In Him, all prophecy came to a head and was consummated. He was "...the one who should come" (Lk 24:25-27). The first name in the New Testament is "Jesus," because the New Testament is prophecy being fulfilled. Names were sometimes changed when a person changed: Abram became Abraham, Jacob became Israel, Naomi said, "call me Mara." It commemorated their new experience. Saul of Tarsus — the man, whose hero was the proud King Saul, became the humble "Paul" when he met Jesus. However, the name of Jesus never changed.

No experience changed Him. He came to save His people from their sins, and He does. Though the name of Jesus was never altered, two titles were added. After His triumph on the cross, Peter announced in Jerusalem, "God has made this same Jesus both Lord and Christ" (Acts 2:36). *Jesus* is His personal name. *Lord* is His rank and office. *Christ* is His work as the One anointed to set the captives free (Is 61:1).

SALVATION SCENARIO

The Lord set up the whole salvation scenario. He not only wrote the play, built the theatre, and choreographed every scene, but was also the chief performer. To save Israel God sent Moses, Joshua, Samson, Gideon, and others. This time, to save us, He sent nobody — He came Himself. He let nothing stand in His way. It meant unspeakable humiliation, Gethsemane, mockery, Calvary, death... All God had and was, He put into the business of saving us. He had no prompting, no example. With a Savior like that, we have full guarantee. "Goodness and mercy shall follow me all the days of my life." (Ps 23:6) Through Isaiah God said "I, even I, am the Lord, and beside me there is no Savior." (Is 43:11) Every Bible page echoes it.

NO BETTER TIMES

Some Christians wait to evangelize till times seem better. The best time is for the worst times. "Now is the day of salvation." (2 Cor 6:2) Today is always the most opportune day. The Holy Spirit is never on vacation. Many are always preparing. The best way to prepare for evangelism is to do it. Conferences, seminars, prolonged prayer sessions may be excellent, but they often produce only perpetual students, not witnesses. They are too busy learning how instead of actually doing it — turning things over in our mind plows no fields. Jesus was unhurried but always urgent. His Word was to preach "I must work the works of Him who sent Me while it is day; the night is coming when no one can work." (Jn 9:4)

A MENU ON ITS OWN NEVER FILLS AN EMPTY STOMACH

Many churches for years have failed to declare the salvation of the Lord. The hungry come but are offered no bread of life, but a diet of straw. All people find is a performance, a ritual, or routine service, with no real word from God. The most gorgeous ceremony never satisfies. It is only a picture of reality. A picture of a good dinner never filled an empty stomach. A symbol of divine truth never filled an empty heart. We need Jesus Himself. He is alive and ready to take over.

PASSION OF GOD

The gospel is the passion of God. Salvation came from the furnace of God's heart. "God so loved the world" (Jn 3:16), and His love burns like a beacon on the hilltop of Calvary. As it declares in Jeremiah 23:29, "Is not my word like fire," declares the Lord, "and like a hammer that breaks a rock in pieces?"

LIKE PORCUPINES, BRISTLING WITH FAULTS

We sin the same old sins, and we need the same old Savior, scientists included, which keeps the newspaper scandal sheets going. The devil hasn't even invented a new sin since the Garden of Eden, nor found a new high-tech stain remover for sinful hearts. Technology provides every comfort except for guilty consciences. The blood of Jesus Christ, God's Son, is still the only cleanser from all unrighteousness. Self-salvation leaves us blundering along like porcupines, bristling with faults.

ANCHOR OF THE SOUL

The cross stands fast. It is an anchor of the soul. That figure of speech is found in the book of Hebrews 6:19-20. "This (hope) we have as an anchor of the soul, both sure and steadfast, and which enters the Presence (behind) the veil, where the forerunner has entered for us, {even} Jesus..." This is a sea-going picture from those ancient days. A ship comes into harbor but cannot draw too near to the shore in the darkness. So, a sailor gets into a boat with an anchor and a line attached which is also fixed to the ship. He is called the "forerunner." As he rows, the line between anchor and ship is played out and links them. Eventually the forerunner boat arrives, and the seaman carries the anchor ashore and secures it on land. In the morning, no sails are needed. The crew of the ship begins to wind in the anchor cable, yet it is not the anchor which moves but the ship. Slowly the vessel winches towards the shore. This is the background to the word "forerunner." Our "forerunner" is Jesus who has entered through the veil and our anchor is made fast. Our salvation is secure like the sailor ashore whom the crew cannot see. Christ is no longer visible to us, He is "ashore" in glory, and we are attached by faith to glory by Him. He has entered glory for us. Day by day the cable is shortening and pulling us nearer and nearer to Christ our forerunner. Eventually we shall reach heaven's shore and what shall we see? Our "forerunner" waiting to greet us, that "where He is there we may also be."

WHAT CHRIST DIED FOR

Jesus Christ did not suffer on a cross to provide careers or jobs for bishops, priests, pastors, or evangelists. He died as He said, "to seek and to save the lost." (Lk 19:10) If Christ had to endure such horror and agony, salvation must be an awesome thing. The cross is the epic scale by which to measure the power and value of our salvation.

KEEPING YOU ON YOUR FEET

You don't have to sit on your salvation as if it would fly away unless you were careful. You don't have to save your salvation. The Lord preserves your soul! "And now to him who can keep you on your feet, standing tall in his bright presence, fresh and celebrating — to our one God, our only Savior, through Jesus Christ, our Master, be glory, majesty, strength, and rule before all time, and now, and to the end of all time. Yes." (Jude 1:24) MSG

SURE-FOOTED

The Lord is sure-footed and never loses track of us. We erect barriers, but He knows the way around them. In the Garden of Eden, God called out to Adam, "Where are you?" (Gen 3:9) Adam did not answer but the Lord found him all the same! He came to seek and to save "completely" (Heb 7:25). That is His great work. He does not save people just for a day or two; He is the author of eternal salvation. "Safe in the arms of Jesus..."

CHRIST'S PULPIT

Calvary was Christ's platform and the cross His pulpit. From it, stained with His life's blood, Jesus proclaims salvation, freedom from sin's chains, healing in sickness, eternal life to all who believe. Nobody in this whole world shall be deprived of this unmatched gospel. "The message of the cross is foolishness to those who are perishing, but to us who are being saved, it is the power of God." (1 Cor 1:18)

THE HIGHEST HONOR

The angel who appeared to Cornelius in Acts, Chapter 10, was not allowed to mention the name of Jesus, or to speak about salvation to the man. That high and holy privilege was (and is) reserved for men and women — people like you and me. All the angel could say was, "Now send men to Joppa, and send for Simon whose surname is Peter." (Acts 10:5) This mighty seraph from the highest heaven had to bow low to Peter's higher privilege.

It pleases God to call and to send people like you and me. It has always been this way. God used four evangelists — Matthew, Mark, Luke, and John — to write down the story of the Gospel of Jesus Christ. Such a pattern is linked in my mind to the four men in Old Testament times who carried the Ark of the Covenant. Carriers of the gospel change from generation to generation, but the gospel remains the same. Now we are here, and today it is our turn. God has called you and me. The gospel needs to be taken to the ends of the earth. This is the Great Commission of the Lord to us — and the King's business requires haste.

WE ARE GOD'S REPORTERS

The cross is central to anything we ever say about God. The God we know is identified by the cross. If Christ died for everyone, then everyone should be told about it. Salvation is perfect and complete. But it needs to be applied like a cure for sin. The gospel cannot operate where it is unknown. We are His reporters, His publishers, and His newsagents.

A NEW DECREE

Jesus "stood and cried." (Jn 7:37) That was very unusual. No rabbi of Israel stood. Usually Jesus did not stand either, but sat to teach, as in the boat and on the mount. People stood in the presence of rabbi teachers out of respect, at least. Jesus is here acting not as a teacher, but as a king standing to give a new decree. When Jesus spoke "it was done, he commanded, and it stood fast." (Ps 33:9) By His word the heavens were made, and now by His word, a new day of wonder and blessing dawns — a new spiritual fact emerges. The Holy Spirit, the Third Person of the Trinity, yields Himself to those who yield themselves to Him. We are still in the day of salvation.

PERMANENT AUTHORITY

The early Christians knew that their permanent authority in Christ did not fluctuate according to their own spiritual condition. Their salvation and faith did not rest in themselves, in their own sufficiency, but on the perfection of their Lord and Savior, Jesus Christ. If they willed to do what He sent them to do, Jesus would always be with them. You and I should not feel different. Jesus is with us *always*.

THE GOD OF COMPASSION

God's commitment to save the world is vital. It is God's own aim and therefore has top priority. The God of all compassion who went to the length of Christ crucified would not hang around waiting until we are all mature and model Christians, sanctified saints before acting. The salvation of the world is too important to be left while we work towards perfection. The truth is that it does not await the spiritual refinement of believers. Piety is not power, holiness is not always zeal, and faith and goodness do not always go hand in hand. Jesus told us to go into all the world with the gospel, not into retreats and cloisters.

RELEASED FROM THE CAGE

A bird born in a cage has no experience with the outside world. It knows nothing about the golden sun, the blue sky, or the lofty mountains. The idea of soaring freely among such beauty would seem like a cruel fantasy. But beyond your cage of sin is a glorious world called The Kingdom of God, and it is no fantasy. It's the real world you yet have never known — a world of sins forgiven, peace with God, and eternal life. The condition? Repent of your sin and receive Jesus Christ as your personal Savior. That will be the moment your cage-door opens, and you are released, saved, set free. Welcome to the Kingdom of God.

SHATTERING BREAKTHROUGH

How does one become a Christian and know God without fear? There are so many current answers — mostly cross-currents, every opinion claiming to be as good as anybody else's. That means they are all equally unsafe and fragile bathtubs to launch out on the Pacific of eternity. A fatal bias bends us off-course. The nightmare proof of it comes with every news bulletin. Thinkers and religionists despair of sin as incurable except through Christianity. Believers enjoy a liberation and an unmistakable consciousness of divine forgiveness. To prove that you are a Christian with a christening certificate is flimsy evidence, like the fig leaves the first sinners, Adam and Eve, wore to meet God. Leaves won't cover our moral nakedness, nor paper leaves, testimonials, résumé records, church membership cards, letters of recommendation, nor our final obituary notices. We Bible-believing Christians are united to this Scripture teaching, that social standing, church membership, Christian work, generosity, sacrifice, or any other self-effort that will never admit us to the Kingdom of God. Virtue brings no complimentary ticket. Positive and objective assurance comes solely by the life, death and resurrection of Christ Jesus our Lord. *His work alone brings us into a happy relationship with God.* We are not nice people a bit dented that can be touched-up, have a few unsociable habits painted out and restored to showroom condition. "We are rebels that need to lay down our arms." Christ's work was a shattering breakthrough. His triumphant cry on the cross reached the heights of heaven's throne, rent the rocks, ripped open the Temple veil, and shook hell. He made the impossible possible. We can be "born-again" as "New creatures in Christ Jesus." How? "Whoever calls on the name of the Lord shall be saved." *Do it now!*

Witnesses

LIVING PIECE OF EVIDENCE

Jesus said, "...and you shall be my witnesses..." (Acts 1:8) Normally a witness only speaks and describes what he has seen. Sometimes however a witness is a piece of evidence. Perhaps a man has been cruelly attacked and injured. He appears in court to display himself — the damage and injury. His scars speak for themselves. He himself is a piece of evidence. We believers are not lawyers, attorneys, or barristers in court pleading in the defense of Jesus. We are witnesses. Witnesses don't argue and don't plead. They simply speak the truth and declare what they know. And here I stand — being a living piece of evidence that Jesus is alive and that there is cleansing power in the blood of Christ.

EACH BELIEVER A WITNESS

There is one gifting for every believer: We are all gifted to witness. But the gift comes with an obligation. We hear much about "giftings." Many want miracle gifts, naturally. But the supreme gift already lies within every born-again Christian. It is Christ in us, the "indescribable gift" (2 Cor 9:15), making each of us a witness.

MATCHING THE MOMENT

A fervent Christian is an opportunist. He doesn't wait for opportunities, he creates them. He doesn't strike the iron *while* it is hot, but *until* it is hot — and then keeps on striking. He doesn't have a glory-party when the walls of Jericho have fallen, but crawls over the rubble, sword in hand, and fights for every home, street, family, and soul. The Apostle Paul was such an opportunist. He was single-minded, innovative, and resourceful, matching the moment with Holy Spirit means. That is a good example to follow.

PULLING THE PLUG

The woman at the Well of Jacob was a quite sociable person. But the heart of the matter is something else. Jesus is not a religionist but a Savior! He didn't come to save religion but to save people! The human heart is like a lake that has been dammed up. We see the beautiful and quiet surface— but Jesus sees more. *He* sees all the garbage and catastrophes at the bottom. "Go and call your husband," He said. (Jn 4:16) The woman got a shock... "This is not church the way I know it!" Jesus told her, "Five husbands you have had...." That moment the Lord pulled the plug which was at the bottom of her heart-lake. This dirty bottom began to empty itself. All uncleanness, adultery, vile lusts, hypocrisy, hate, injustice, fraud, lies, thieving, unrighteousness, and deception were drained and replenished with living, sparkling water — *life, health, and peace* flowed in! All dead works were flushed out and she was set free. Please listen, Jesus didn't come to shame sinners — Jesus came to save sinners! Jesus died for us! He has not come like a policeman to arrest us — He sets us free! *He* is the mighty Savior.

MIND IN THE BEGINNING WHAT MATTERS IN THE END

We were in a pastor's prayer-meeting on our knees. Next to me knelt a dear old servant of God and I couldn't help but overhear what he prayed: "Lord, forgive me where I have allowed unclean things in my life." This moved me deeply. I was still a young man in my twenties and followed it up with my own prayer, "Lord, when I am old, I never want to have to pray like that. Please help me to mind in the beginning what matters in the end." It is so important to live a holy life in the name of Jesus.

WE HAVE PETER'S KEYS

Jesus gave the Apostle Peter the keys of the Kingdom, but those keys are not jangling from Peter's belt at the Pearly Gates. They are the gospel of Christ crucified, and the Holy Spirit. Peter used them first, that's all, and today *we have the same keys* (Matt 16:19). Peter saw what nobody on earth had ever seen before — 3000 people being born-again by the Holy Spirit on one day. (Acts 2) Then the apostles went out and proved the power of those keys. The dead were raised, the deaf, blind, and crippled restored, and multitudes turned to Jesus. A new thing arose in the world, the church of Jesus Christ. So, it is today. We see crowds stretching to the horizon, masses of people never seen before — ready to repent and believe. The gospel-keys are working nowadays even more effective than ever before.

ACCENT OF FAITH

There is an imperative in the heart of Jesus which transfers itself to those who belong to Him. We are here on earth in His place. He said, "You did not choose me, but I chose you and appointed you to go and bear fruit, fruit that will last." (Jn 15:16) Our business is not to be busy but to witness. Wherever we are, what we are doesn't change. An American is an American, whatever he does or wherever he goes. He has a living to earn, a family to support, perhaps a business to run, and he can be identified all over the world because he speaks English with an American accent. Christians are Christ's witnesses in the same way. We are what we are. At all times, our lifestyle and accent of faith reveal to whom we belong. We belong to Christ.

NO TWISTED TYPE OF FAITHFULNESS

We need more imaginative approaches in soul-winning, rather than people doing things by "tried and proven" methods — even methods I have tried and proven. Methods which have made little impact in the past are not likely to produce an impact now. Plodding along "mechanically" might be called faithfulness, but our primary concern in evangelism is effectiveness, not this twisted type of faithfulness.

Faith

END OF FANTASY AND BEGINNING OF REALITY

Faith in God is not fantasy; it is the end of fantasy. Faith does not end in faith, but in reality and blessing. Some accuse us of "preaching an emotional gospel." Well, the truth is that it cannot be avoided! If the gospel is not emotional then nothing ever was. "Sensational gospel?" *God* made it sensational! When the preacher appeals to "believe in Him who raises the dead and calls those things which are not as though they were" — surely it is a sensation!

THE ABC OF FAITH

The ABCs of faith are that as we act God acts. You simply do what should be done when you know that you can't succeed unless God helps you. The whole Bible is written to break down unbelief and build up our trust in God.

THE COMING DAWN

The Lord Jesus was the one whom everyone could fling his or her arms around. His mother, Mary, did and so did Mary Magdalene, who was saved by the loving touch of the Master (Matt 27:56-61). In the Old Testament, revelation came to people about God, but it seemed to be only to rare individuals, such as Abraham, Jacob, and the prophets. The masses moved very slowly — and often moved backward. God used various circumstances and methods to help them to have faith. But the coming of Jesus swept the world. Somehow, Calvary does what the awesome manifestations of Sinai couldn't do. Jesus is the great Creator of faith. Looking back over the long, cheerless world history of uncertainty and doubt, we can see when it changed. It came with the gospel. It awakened sleeping trust. The dawn had come.

WHAT CAN GO WRONG CAN GO RIGHT

If Jesus, the Lord of miracles, was around, walking miraculously on the water, then Peter was not about to miss his chance. Other miracles could happen. Why let Him pass by? Peter certainly did not. Unfortunately, people do let the Lord of miracles pass by. If there is a Jesus, why live as if there were not? If there is a Father in heaven, why live like orphans? If there is a Savior, why die unsaved? If there is a healer, why not ask Him to heal? If there is an all-sufficient Christ, why scratch and scrape like chickens in a farmyard? If things can go wrong, they can go right. If the devil can work, so can God. How many people expect it? Faith is for the day of calamity, but that is when some believers stop believing. Their faith only flourishes in glorious meetings. They wear their life jackets on deck but throw them away when they fall into the sea. So, Peter went in for a miracle. Live by faith! That is life as God meant it to be. Miracles come to those who live the way of faith. That is God's grand design for our lives, for us to step out, depending on the Word of God and the power of God to give us miracles. We cannot walk with God without experiencing wonders.

BIGGER ALPHABET AND BETTER LANGUAGE

When it comes to the Lord, human language is never good enough. The first Christians had to give new meaning to many words and even coin new words, because Jesus did new things and was a new kind of person. God did not communicate about Himself with mere words. He simply presented Himself with His actions, and to describe Him we often need a bigger alphabet and better language. When we speak of God, we frequently lack the words. God never relied on mere words to inspire our faith in Him. To show us who and what He is, He came! "The Word became flesh and dwelt among us," the Gospel of John says, "and we beheld His glory, the glory as of the only begotten of the Father, full of grace and truth" (1:14). God is the eternal unchanging One. "For I am the Lord," the book of Malachi says. "I do not change" (3:6). He is now and always has been.

LANGUAGE MUST BE PUSHED AROUND

God backs up His faithfulness in this text in the words, "I am the Alpha and the Omega, the Beginning and the End, says the Lord, who is and who was and who is to come, the Almighty." (Rev. 1:8) This is an unusual usage, for instead of, "who is to come," we would have typically said, "who will be"— using the verb, "to be." God used "to be" twice in "who was, and is," then switched to a different verb and used, "to come." Why this peculiar way of putting it? The reason is that God is "unusual." He baffles grammar and syntax, and the language must be pushed around when we speak of Him. Christ Himself was a mystery, as He attests in Scripture, "All things have been delivered to Me by My Father, and no one knows the Son except the Father. Nor does anyone know the Father except the Son, and the one to whom the Son wills to reveal Him." (Matt. 11:27) To talk about Him in ordinary language always leaves something out.

NOT CHOICE — BUT CHOSEN

Israel bought freedom at a knock-down price, but they soon doubted the bargain. "We remember the fish which we ate freely in Egypt. The cucumbers, the melons, the leeks, the onions, and the garlic." (Num 11:5). Cucumbers! A lure back to the iron furnace of slavery? Cucumbers — yet they were the chosen agents introducing the greatest change in history. Leading a new and fundamental new order of life for man on earth. God had come down from heaven and made them "a chosen generation, a royal priesthood, a holy nation, His own special people." (1 Peter 2:9) But, inexplicably their minds were on cucumbers. Israel did not choose the Lord, but the Lord chose them. They were not choice but chosen (Deut 7:7). Escaping Egypt's grinding slavery, they left Egypt with backpacks, a dozen restless clans, and unreliable, superstitious, worshipers of Egyptian gods. The Lord led them with favor and infinite patience and showed them how to live. He commissioned them with a national purpose. A purpose beyond their own self-preservation that no other nation can claim even now, nearly 4,000 years later. What a wonderful Lord.

THE FERTILE GROUND

Seeking God's Kingdom, we must have faith, for
faith is the fertile ground in which God moves. He plants
qualities in the man or woman of faith, which soon become
admired wherever. Little people take on stature by faith in
Christ. They have zest, a grip on life, and tackle difficulties with
determination and confidence. It is common for believers to
perform beyond their natural capacity. Jesus said to the unlearned
fisher lads on the Sea of Galilee, "Follow Me, and I will make you
fishers of men." (Matt. 4:19) They switched direction and elevation
as they became His apostles. So, can we.

SOMEBODY TO TRUST

Faith is not just believing there is a God. We must trust
Him. When I get on a plane, I believe there is a pilot of course,
but if for any reason I could not trust him I would quickly walk
off again. I must believe *in* him. James takes us back to some of
the first principles of the life of Jesus. He wrote about faith. He
said "You believe that there is one God. Good! Even the demons
believe that and shudder," but — they remained demons. (Jas
2:19) Christians look to "Jesus, the author and finisher of their
faith..." (Heb 12:2) Jesus did not give us something to believe, *but
somebody to trust*. Christianity keeps an ancient creed but believes
a *person*. You can't sign on the dotted line to make yourself a
Christian. You cannot utter a formal sentence to get converted. It
is a matter of the heart, resting on Christ, moment by moment, and
being led by His precious Holy Spirit.

FAITH IN GOD NEVER DIES
A NATURAL DEATH

Faith in God never dies a natural death. It doesn't die easily either. We must work at it. We are surrounded everyday by doubters. Godlessness is the order of the day. Newspapers, radio, and television push unbelief down our throats for breakfast, lunch, and dinner. Try a different diet — start believing! Put your faith in Jesus. Come exercising faith, hopefully, however nervously, and you will get more faith. "Whoever has, will be given more," Christ said.

NO COMFORT IN UNBELIEF

I find no comfort in uncertainty. I face the wild waters of the future and cannot launch my eternal soul on a raft of guesswork and human opinion. Like Paul, however, I do say "I know whom I have believed," (2 Tim 1:12) *it is Jesus!*

MOST DANGEROUS UNBELIEF

Syrians besieged Samaria, causing catastrophic starvation and Israel almost surrendered. But *Elisha* was there, God's speaker with an unalterable Word from the Lord. (2 Kings 7:1-2 and 16-18) A debate ensued between the two speakers — *God's* and the governments, Elisha and the king's representative. God's Speaker (Elisha) said, "Tomorrow will be plenty of food in the Gate of Samaria." The king's speaker replied, "Impossible, even if God would make windows in heaven." God's Speaker, "You shall see it but not eat from it." Then the Syrians fled and left plenty of free food. A riot of Faith followed. Please note, the government speaker was trampled to death by people who rushed to the gate of Samaria to get the food he had chosen not believe in. This perfectly describes how dangerous unbelief is. When God speaks, we must listen and obey. You better believe it.

THE BADGE OF FAITH

Bible faith is not a subject like gardening, sports, or photography just for those interested. We either believe or perish. Faith is a universal human requirement and responsibility. This is set out by Jesus in the parable of the wedding feast in Matthew 22:12. All guests were provided with a wedding garment, meaning faith. One man came wearing his own clothes, apparently thinking that he could dress better than anybody else. He was thrown out. The standard dress in the Kingdom of God is faith. "Without faith it is impossible to please God." (Heb 11:6) This one individual had come to the feast proud and superior, not wearing the garments of God-given faith. Heaven will not be monopolized by theological graduates, nor by people who have, "never robbed a bank," but only by people displaying the simple badge of faith, being saved by God's grace.

GOD IS NOT THE "GREAT I WAS" BUT THE "GREAT I AM"

"Now faith is...." we read in Hebrews 11: 1, but then it goes on using examples of the *past*. Should He not have written "Now faith *was*"? Here is a wonderful truth, *faith* is always

in the present tense, because God is always in the present indicative. Faith is always in the *now*, because God is simply a *now-God*. He says, "I am that I am." (Exod 3:14) He's not the Great *I was*, but the Great *I am*! The Bible was not written to just to tell us what God *can* do, but what God *will* do. Through it we come to *know* Jesus! This knowledge brings *trust*, which is faith! How wonderful.

CAN WE LIMIT GOD?

Whatever power God gives us it is subject to faith. *All* power is available. It either operates or is limited by our faith. There is no point in praying for more power, more Holy Spirit. He does not come in degrees, but in fullness, "according to your faith be it unto you." The limitation is not in God — He comes to us in fullness. We limit God. Nowhere in Scripture is power spoken of in degree. The Holy Spirit is the One all-sufficient power. He can be grieved and quenched, but not by the world because the world hasn't got the Spirit. Only Christians can grieve the Spirit, and that is by unbelief, because unbelief ties the hands of God.

WISHBONE OR BACKBONE

Some have wishes. Others, like Joshua, have purposes. A whole generation of Israel wished, and died still wishing. They had a wishbone, but no backbone. By faith in God Joshua turned "wishes" into land, cities, homes, and possessions. I mean that faith in God produces concrete results.

WHEN WE BELIEVE, WE DARE

James 2:26 says, "...faith without works is dead." It is not good to say, I believe the Lord is with me, if you never go anywhere for Him. If you never place yourself in a position where you must depend on God, your faith is hollow. Your belief may be very positive, but it is a dead positive if you do not act on it. Deeds come alive with faith, and faith comes alive with deeds. Believing goes on in the heart and mind, unseen, until it translates into something we do. The power of God operates when we operate by faith. The famous chapter of Hebrews 11 was written to show that because the ancients of faith believed, they dared. Let us dare to do something special for Jesus.

THE BIBLE — THE BOOK OF THE BOLD

Faith breeds boldness. The leading men in Jerusalem, "...saw the courage of Peter and John." (Acts 4:13) Their fearlessness was plain for all to see. Israel's supreme judges with their fossilized traditions were shocked into wide-eyed disbelief at the sight of mere Galilean fishermen addressing the court with the confidence of kings issuing edicts. The Bible is the book of the bold, not the cringing. In fact, its final warning is to "...the cowardly and the unbelieving..." (Rev 21:8). Scripture presents us with the fearless, who dared to go where no one else would and to do what no one dreamed possible. Radicals? Of course, they were! It takes radicals to change the world.

THE OPPOSITE OF FEAR

The opposite of fear is not fearlessness or courage, but *faith*. We are not told to "pull up our socks," but "In what time I am afraid I will trust and not be afraid."(Ps 56:3) Fear won't help us, but faith in God will. Put your trust in Jesus.

FAITH CANCELS FEAR

"By faith Moses, when he was born, was hidden three months by his parents, because they saw he was a beautiful child; and they were not afraid of the king's command." (Heb. 11:23) Just think of what that involved. The Egyptian state and Pharaoh, its head, had made it illegal to keep a Hebrew baby-boy. By law, such children were to be killed at birth. Soldiers moved around to carry out this order. What terror and grief there must have been! Then Moses was born. His parents looked upon this lovely son and were determined to defy the law and hide the baby. "By faith . . . they were not afraid." Officers of the law were around, and their footsteps were heard stopping at their very door, seeking the child's life! Who would not shake in their shoes if armed men were waiting, ordered to kill their baby? Yet, "...they were not afraid." This is a glorious truth: *Faith Cancels fear*. Their faith may have looked naive and foolish. But the situation was exactly what God likes. He delights to do the impossible.

THE DIFFERENCE BETWEEN A WASH AND A WASH

In John, Chapter 9, a blind man had to find his way still sightless after leaving Jesus. He was told to go to the pool of Siloam and wash. It was an act of blind faith, literally, but it brought him a miracle, "...and he came seeing," (v. 7). "Believe!" says Jesus, and we stand shivering on the bank of the river as if to plunge in would be the death of us. It turns out to be life. The leap into the darkness is a leap into the light. When you are believing you are seeing. Every day many other people washed themselves in Siloam, but no miracle happened. And as there was a difference between a wash and a wash, so there is also a difference between faith and faith.

MUTUAL TRUST

Personal relationships cannot exist without faith. Friendships are formed by mutual trust. God invites us to relate to Him as a friend. As the Bible says, "...without faith it is impossible to please Him." (Heb 11:6) With someone having counted 7847 Divine promises, the Bible assures us of God's competency and goodwill. We may know what somebody was in the past, but for what he will be in the future, we can only trust. Knowing what God has done assures us of His character. But the future is a matter of trust. The Bible's central verse and message is, "It is better to trust in the Lord than to put confidence in man." (Ps 118:8)

THERE MUST BE A RESPONSE

Faith is much more than just knowledge of Christ. There must be a response to that belief system. Do we do what we believe? If we believe in a seed, we plant it and patiently wait for it to grow. A man who owns an airplane but won't risk flying is contrary to a pilot's character. And believing in God without expectation that He will really do something is contrary to the entire Bible's message. Faith is appropriation. "Lord I believe..."

DO THE WILL OF GOD

This world has false standards, false values, false gods, and false heroes. Its honor is a wreath of fading fame. True greatness is not bigness or spiritual prominence. It is to do God's will! We have one lifetime only to reach our own generation with the gospel. Each believer reaching others is the secret of expansion, and always has been, but "...by all means save some."

FAITH IS WHAT WE DO

Faith doesn't come in sizes like suit jackets. Let's not confuse faith with virtue. Faith is there. Faith is just faith. Virtue is developed. Faith doesn't come as does learning the piano grade by grade. We can have faith even when we know we are not very good. Nonbelievers can have faith, otherwise they could never be brought to the realization that Jesus Christ is Lord. Faith is not what we *say*, Faith is what we *do*. Doers of the Word of God are the true believers.

THE GOSPEL TRUMPET HAS NO STICKY VALVE

When you are saved, you should know it. Otherwise, how can you be a witness for Christ? The Bible speaks clearly and positively — it does not stammer. When you read it, you become certain! The Holy Spirit writes no doubts. The promises of God are Yes and Amen (2 Cor 1:20) and not no or maybe. The gospel trumpet has no sticky valve and sounds no faltering note. When an earthquake shook the Philippian jail and all who were in it, the jailor cried out, "What must I do to be saved?" Paul did not say, "Well, what do you think? Do you have any idea yourself?" He made a firm statement of fact in Acts 16:31: "Believe on the Lord Jesus Christ, and you will be saved." The gospel is God's message, not just Christian opinion.

APPROPRIATE THE PROMISE

Many wait as obedient servants, and they do just that — wait, but take no action because they have no leading. Half the idleness of the Christian church arises from the desire to be obedient and "not get ahead of God," as if they could. But the great saints of God, from biblical times through to today, put their own finger on the promises of God to go ahead, and that is how the work of God has progressed. The Word of God is not some subjective impulse, but our authority for action. Jonathan had no special word or prompting from God. He simply decided to trust God and have a go. On his own initiative he emerged... A skirmish took place and God was with Jonathan. Today God calls out across the world, across the churches, and says, "Go!" If anybody volunteers, He goes with them like His favored friends.

FAITH CAN SNAP US OUT

We can fail in living while succeed in making a living — a good living and a poor life. But "godliness is profitable for all things, having promise of the life that now is and of that which is to come." (1 Tim 4:8) Faith can snap us out of our snug little burrows and get us going for God.

NO SQUEEZING

Some people are full of money as a tube is full of toothpaste, but squashing will only produce a tiny something. Our God is the source of all riches but needs *no* pressure. The knowledge of the riches of Christ are not merely academic, a statistical fact for the books. He says, "Ask and you shall receive…" (Jn 16:24) No pressure! No pleading, just receiving!

ONLY GOD'S WILL IS POSSIBLE

Let us enter the Garden of Gethsemane with humble awe. The Son of God is praying about what is possible, and what He says penetrates to the very heart of the matter. Jesus said, "O My Father, if it is possible, let this cup pass from Me; nevertheless, not as I will, but as You will." (Matt 26:39) We understand from this that only that which is God's will is possible. A disciple who heard Jesus in the Garden later wrote, "If we ask anything according to

His will, He hears us." (1 Jn 5:14) God's Word is God's Will. Read it. He will speak to you.

FAITH – THE QUALIFYING FACTOR

With God, *faith* is the qualifying factor. He places His resources at our disposal. God did not honor the famous characters in Scripture because of their own natural greatness, nor for their moral greatness. The lifestyle of most of them would shock us today. Saul was more moral than David, but God chose David, because David was a faith-activist. It isn't even "great" faith He wants, just simple "everyday-faith." Jesus called His disciples "Little-Faiths," (Matt 8:26) yet He chose them and made them the most effectual figures of history. Compared to the resources open to us in God, our natural abilities are a drop in the ocean. But our own limitations mean nothing to Him. When we have faith, gifted or not, we stand at the threshold of great usefulness.

FAITH GIVES LIFE VALIDITY AND VITALITY

God had made the first man, Adam, and then He made the first civilized man, Abraham. The latter gave us the greatest discovery of all time, *faith*, the key to unlock the secrets of life, whether for individuals, nations, or empires. Abraham was the original man to use that key and open the treasure house of divine blessing and help. He is called "the father of all who believe." (Rom 4:11) Without that key the blue-print of the Creator is locked away. If we build without the architect, our progress always proves to be a stairway of sand. The Psalmist wrote, "Unless

the Lord builds the house its builders labor in vain." (Ps 127:1)
Faithless life is lifeless life. Faith makes life live. "He that believes,
has life. He that does not believe has no life." Faith gives life
vitality. Faith gives life validity. "Only believe."

"ONLY BELIEVE"

Jesus said, "Fear not! Only believe!" (Lk 8:50) Why
did He use the word "only?" Well, at birth God has given to
every human being the ability to believe — just watch a little child.
It is simple. When you are hungry, only eat. When you are thirsty
only drink. When you are tired only sleep. And when you need a
miracle from God, Jesus opens His arms and says, "only believe."
You got it? Practice it.

SPARK OF FAITH

Once old car-engines sparked and got the magneto
going. The magneto, in turn, kept the engine going. It just
needed the rider's first effort to start up. That is also a picture of
faith. Faith works when you go, and you go by faith. You begin
and live by faith. Jesus said, "To him that has shall more be given."
(Lc 19:26) Begin with what spark of faith you have and more will
be given. There is no need to run anxiously to every conference
and seminar to find the secret. Don't just go *to* God but go *for* God!

LEARN TO LEAN

*B*ible people struggled with God's goodness and the problem of evil. Their story helps us in the good fight of faith. They learned to lean on God. In fact, Israel was the most harried and persecuted race on earth, yet it was Israel who gave us the most glorious recommendation to trust in God. "When you pass through the waters, I will be with you; and ...the rivers... will not sweep over you. When you walk through the fire, you will not be burned... For I am the Lord your God, the Holy One of Israel, your Savior." (Is 43:2-3) After 3,000 years Israel is still present, and their God is also our God.

IDENTIFYING JESUS

The disciples saw Jesus walk on the water and were scared (Matt 14:25-29). Peter cried "Lord *if* it is you, ask me to come..." He wanted proper identification. Peter knew that the Lord usually commands the impossible and then makes it possible. If it was "his" Jesus, He would do just that. And then indeed, Peter challenged Jesus to challenge him. With it he touched the heart of God.

GOD IS NO DEMOCRAT

*G*od is not a democrat — He is a theocrat. Because of Israel's doubts He dropped a whole generation and stuck with only two people. The rest died in the desert of doubt. He stood with merely two believing men: Joshua and Caleb! This is how serious God takes unbelief. Let's decide today to trust the Lord no matter what.

BUSINESS WITH GOD

When we do business with people, we need money. When we do business with God, we need faith. Faith is the currency of the Kingdom of God.

GOD NEVER FORGETS HIS PROMISES

God never forgets His promises, and they are not cancelled by the death of their first recipient(s). He promised things to Moses, that he never began to enjoy. But it had revealed God's will in the matter, and the same thing would be done for Joshua. If God's promises apply to our situation, then they are promises as much to us as to the original beneficiary.

FAITH TAKES A "CHANCE"

Jacob had a breakthrough-experience with God. It not only established a new relationship with God, but it changed his very name to Israel. Gideon, a frustrated farmer, and another doubter stepped out in boldness relying on God, with benefits to the nation. Long afterwards, on the beach of Lake Galilee, Jesus met seven downhearted disciples, re-ordered their steps, and set them going to change the whole world. In Ephesians 1, Paul prays for the believers to experience a breakthrough to see what is the "exceeding greatness" open to them. These people took a chance on God. They were not always believers, but they said, "I will trust God." They took a small step which proved to be a giant stride into a new way of life for them and even for generations to come. I say, "took a chance," but it was only in the way a husband takes a chance on his wife at some special time. He knows her and is sure of her. He exhibits a trust in her that could give her real pleasure. And "without faith it is impossible to please God." That is the kind of "chance" faith takes. Millions live like that today. "The just shall live by faith," the Bible says, not just exist by faith. It involves taking a chance, or it wouldn't be faith. It is confident anticipation based on the knowledge of what God is. Peter knew what Jesus was like and obeyed Him to walk on the water. Faith is to act on the strength of what we know, expecting God to be to us what we know He is. When we "risk" everything on God, He proves to be faithful, today.

LOGIC OF FAITH

Bible prophets only declared the mind of God. They were not thinkers, drawing their own conclusions. They simply said what God told them to say. Listen how Peter put it, "We have the prophetic word confirmed, which you do well to heed as a light that shines in a dark place ... for prophecy never came by the will of man, but holy men of God spoke as they were moved by the Holy Spirit" (2 Pet 1:19-21). This is emphasized in the story of the corrupt prophet Balaam. He said, "Though Balak were to give me his house full of silver and gold, I could not go beyond the word of the Lord my God, to do less or more." (Num 22:18) When Israel hesitated between two opinions, the logic of Joshua's solution could not have been simpler; "If God is God," he said, "then serve Him" (Josh 22:5)

THE HEART OF THE MATTER

Faith is a personal relationship, not a mathematical relationship between numbers. We know what God did yesterday, but we must trust Him for tomorrow. Faith is akin to love. It is a heart matter. We do not decide to fall in love after weighing all the pros and cons. Couples get married on trust, not on scientific evidence or conclusive logic.

FAITH RELATES US TO GOD

God took Abraham's name as part of His name! He called Himself the "the God of Abraham!" The Almighty identified Himself with a man. It meant that the reputation of God rested on Abraham. What God was like, a new God to the world in general, would be assumed from what Abraham was like. God risked His name by joining it with Abraham. Abraham believed in the Lord, the Lord believed in Abraham. Something similar is reflected in what Jesus said in Matthew 10:32, "Whoever acknowledges me before men, I will also acknowledge him before my Father in heaven." That's the inner truth about faith. It is not merely for getting things or doing things or being something. It relates us to God. Faith is fellowship and is always the condition for our relationship with God. He puts faith in our hearts, and then He puts His faith in us to do His will. It is the faith of God.

THE FAITH-PIVOT

We can switch direction from unbelief to certainty. Faith is a decision. It has happened to many people, like a miracle. It reminds me of the healing of the cripple at the Beautiful Gate. His spiritual feet and ankle bones received strength and they entered the temple, "walking, leaping and praising God" — dancing on faith legs! What a victorious pathway. The Apostle Paul said, "The life I now live, I live by the faith of the Son of God." (Gal 2:20) As this faith-pivot of life swings round, personality is re-molded and our outlook revolutionized. Nothing, simply nothing can re-shape life like faith in God.

IMMUNE SYSTEM CALLED FAITH

Faith is a kind of immune system filtering out fears that otherwise would paralyze all activity. When it fails, we develop all kinds of phobias and compulsions. It is a nervous breakdown. Jesus said not to have phobia but faith (Lk 8:50). Stop using this faculty of faith and you would never get out of bed in the morning or step outside. You might think that the sky could fall. In this world a million cobra troubles are coiled to strike, but we carry on, usually quite regardless and confident. The Bible says that God has dealt to each one a measure of faith (Rom 12:3). Christ said, "Only believe" (Mk 5:36), because we can. Faith is the victory.

CONDUCTIVITY

Have you ever seen a mustard seed? You may need a magnifying glass to see it. But the people to whom Jesus spoke knew seeds. It was an agricultural world. Jesus spoke their farming language. Today, we are a high-tech society, and our expressions are scientific. Jesus spoke the language of the people, and today our expressions come from technology. No doubt today, Jesus would use our common speech. Jesus spoke 2,000 years ago about the mustard seed, a small thing with mighty potency. Maybe today He would talk about a microchip or fuse to illustrate His teaching. "If you have faith as small as an electric fuse, you could transplant trees from soil to sea." Like the mustard seed, the value of a fuse is not in breadth or length. The key is "conductivity." Faith transfers the power of God to wherever it is needed. (Lk 17:6) A fuse is made of a metal, such as silver wire, which offers low resistance to current. Low resistance means high conductivity. Translated into spiritual terms: The lower our resistance to the Word of God, the higher the operational power of God. The higher our resistance to the Word the lower the operational power of God. "Lord I believe!"

FLICK THE SWITCH

Many believe in the work of the Holy Spirit! They preach about it. They rejoice when things happen, but they never get around practicing faith for themselves. They are longing for the power, but never put the plug into the socket. They never 'flick' the switch, and therefore they never tap into the spiritual power lines that are humming night and day. All those human explanations, plausible reasons, generally known sayings, negative teachings, and religious hair-splitting destroy the conductivity of the Word of God. Many know the biblical truths, but never experience them for themselves. It is quite possible for the divine power lines to be severed by human thinking. The Bible gives the following warning, "...but the word which they heard did not profit them, not being mixed with faith in those who heard it." (Heb 4:2) The Bible is given precisely to create faith in its own truth, the greatness of God. Read it! To sing in church, "How great Thou art" is ridiculous if a single molehill is not moved, and every mountain triggers alarm. Trust in God is the power-switch!

TRUMPET OF FAITH

Before Joseph died in Egypt, he took an oath from his children that they take his "bones in a coffin" on the day of departure for the Promised Land. (Gen 50:22-26) Joseph didn't want to be a mummy in Egypt with a private pyramid. He wanted to be present when God opened the Red Sea. They took his bones when they left Egypt (Heb 11:22). The bones didn't rattle in the box, they must have laughed and rejoiced... There was more life in those bones then in those who carried them. The bones arrived, but not the original bearers. Joseph blew the first trumpet of faith for the return of Israel, about 400 years before it happened! He blew it with those not yet born, but who would blow the trumpets to bring down the walls of Jericho. Joseph died at 110 years-old. A man of faith at 110 is younger than a critical teenager! Want to join Joseph's battalion?

MOSES' STAFF

God parted the Red Sea when Moses *had the faith to lift his staff*. God took Isaiah when he volunteered to serve the Lord despite his unclean lips. Jesus said, "They shall lay hands upon the sick…" (Mk 16:18) Well, here are *our* most ordinary hands, but by using them, satanic power is broken TODAY. "My power is made perfect in weakness." (2 Cor 12:9)

FAITH IS TRUST IN GOD

Faith is not a mental exercise to believe the impossible, for example believing what we know is not true. It is not believing "something" at all. Faith is trust in God. It is personal. In the Gospels Jesus never talks about believing something will happen, a miracle perhaps, but always about believing Him. Our destiny rests on faith. We are saved by faith. "Whoever believes in the Son has eternal life." (Jn 3:36) The God we are to trust in is worthy as the God who loved us and gave His Son to bear our sins on the cross.

FAITH IS NOT ARROGANT

Meekness is the astonishment of a man at what God has done for him. Jesus said, "I am meek" (Matt 11:19) His meekness consisted of the fact, that although He was God — He humbled Himself and took upon Himself "the form of a servant." Meekness is an attitude of the Holy Spirit which cancels the thought forever that, "Ye shall be as gods." (Gen 3:5)

Prayer

EVANGELISM PLUS INTERCESSION

The subject of intercession is sacred ground — ground wet with the tears of men and women of God. Jesus Himself has been here, too, in the garden of Gethsemane, praying for us. He is our great teacher. Intercession is not a replacement for soul-winning, because the two of them actually go together. Intercession means telling God about the lost — praying that He will save them from their sins. Evangelism means telling the lost about God — calling them to be reconciled to Him, to stop being His enemies and to become His friends. Intercession and evangelism need each other! Together they carry the gospel into the world.

GOOD REASON FOR PRAYER

When we pray, we pray on the same basis and with the same rights as Paul, John, James, and Peter. We rank equal with the greatest saints. The promises to them are the promises to us. They prayed the same Lord's Prayer as we pray. We have the same privileges as they had. God has no favorites except that we are *all* His favorites. They had the same key to the door as we have — the name of Jesus. We come to the front door and walk in, without knocking, without a receptionist to announce us. We do not need angels or saints to usher us into God's presence. We are sons and heirs — we have complete freedom of access into our Father's house. That is a very good reason indeed for praying. Prayed today?

OPEN HEAVEN

When Jesus *ascended* to heaven, He went through the gate of glory — and left it open. Ten days later the Holy Spirit *descended* through the same opening (Acts 2:1-4). When Stephen was martyred, he said "Look! I see heavens open and the Son of Man standing at the right hand of God." (Acts 7:56) That Gate was *still open* five chapters later — and has *remained open ever since*. We need *not* pray for an open heaven ever again. *It is open!*

PRAYER IS NOT JUST WORDS

Prayer is not just words. It is our spirit making live contact with God's Spirit. Life flows constantly from God like light from the sun. In prayer, we expose ourselves to its rays and sunbathe in the warmth of divine love. We absorb His goodness. It penetrates to the core of our existence. It is life from above.

IS GOD SILENT?

"The silence of God" has been a popular theme, but it misrepresents God. Christ's name, "The Word," hardly suggests a silent God. In Acts 2:4 they spoke, but He gave them utterance — a noise directly echoing God's noise. We read that it attracted an enormous crowd. There was motion and commotion.

WHAT BARE HANDS CAN DO

Murderous bands of Amalekite plunderers began to harass Israel's flanks, picking off stragglers and stripping them of their meager belongings. Joshua had to marshal what men and arms he could. It was a pitiful show since they did not have so much as a rag raised on a banner-pole to rally them. However, Moses had his own bare hands to raise to the God of Heaven, and the Amalekites were routed. Moses said, "Hands were lifted up to the throne of the Lord..." (Ex 17:16) Try it. It really works. Even today.

NOT AN INTERVIEW

Prayer is not an interview with God that terminates when you say, "Amen." It doesn't mean, "So long, Lord!" He is as much with you when you are not praying as when you are. "I will never leave thee nor forsake thee." (Josh 1:5) "Lo! I am with you always." (Matt 28:20) His presence is unconditional with those who love Him.

PRAYER WITH OTHERS

Our Father hears us when we are in tune with the keynote of his purposes. Then we can be sure He hears us. Imagine a violin player who begins his concert performance. The violin sounds beautiful, and the player is clearly a skilled performer — but then suddenly the rest of the orchestra joins in and it is a disaster. What has gone wrong? It's simple — even though the violin is beautiful on its own, it is completely out of tune with the other instruments. Even when all the correct notes are being played, the result sounds terrible. Your prayer might sound excellent, but is it in tune with the will of God? You keep in tune by reading and knowing the Word of God.

WHAT GOD DOES NOT DO

Although the Father sent the Son, and the Son could truly say "I do always those things which the Father does," there was one thing He did that the Father did not do — *pray!* However faithfully we devote ourselves to God, prayer and intercession remains a necessity. The world *must* be prayed for. It is part of the job! It is as much the work of God for us as it was for Christ in His work. The work and the will of God can only be carried out by intercessors. People who work but never intercede don't so much walk along with God as limp along with God.

SECRET PRAYER IS THE SECRET OF PRAYER

Secret prayer is the secret of prayer. Jesus said, "When you pray, go into your room, close the door and pray to your Father, who is unseen." (Matt 6:6) Close the door of your prayer room, and the door of heaven opens. When the 120 disciples locked themselves in, the windows of glory were unlocked, and the Holy Spirit rained upon them (Acts 2). The devil will try to stop you from praying because prayer stops him. All around the world, there are prayer rooms, upper rooms, in churches, colleges, even in administrative offices. They are typical places full of the gospel and Christians. A prayer room is a power house. "Pray without ceasing..." today. (1 Thess 5:17)

PRESENT AND FUTURE SPIRIT-FILLED

What God was and did, spells out His will for the present and future. It is for our faith to grasp it, act upon it and bring to bear God's wonder-working power again upon the world. His past predicts the present — if we believe. There is perfect harmony and consistency in God from eternity to eternity. And it is that eternity which has swept down upon us earthlings and will carry us along in His everlasting joy.

PRAYER HAS BEEN CALLED "QUITE TIME"

The Bible says, "Put on Christ." Christ is not famous for calm composure. His prayers in the Garden, and His road to the cross were no casual affairs. To be like Him would not make a man a model of cool indifference. When Christ entered the Temple, His zeal for God's house made bold men flee. Striding later towards Jerusalem, we read that His very bearing astonished the disciples. His eyes filled with tears as He saw the un-championed multitudes. He was shaken visibly by incredible compassion. Prayer time has been called our quiet time, but His "quiet time" consisted of strong crying, tears, the agony of sweating blood, until angels had to support Him. Love? ...He died for us! That's His sort of love. "Love so amazing, so divine, demands my life, my soul, my all."[4]

THE FAITH OF THE SAINTS

We do not take the gospel-message to the educators of this fallen world and submit to their correction. Paul knew well what a mistake that was, and admonished Timothy to "Preach the word, for the time will come when they will not endure sound doctrine." (2 Tim 4:3) Our message, he said, was not "of man," something thought up, but it was of God, and was put into our hands as a sacred trust, as "towards of the mysteries of God." Christianity does not permit modification and modernization. It is "the faith once delivered to the saints." (Jude 1:3)

GOD'S TELEPHONE NUMBER

When I was still a teenager, I helped my father in his church as a Sunday School teacher. One Sunday I said to my class of boys and girls, "Today I want to give you God's telephone number." Perplexed they asked, "What is His number?" I told them that it was 5015 and they wanted to know where I had got it from. My response was, "From Psalm 50 Verse 15, where God says, 'Call upon me in the day of trouble and I will deliver you.'" One boy of about 12 years jumped up and ran out. 15 minutes later he came back and shouted, "I did it, I did it, I did it!" I said, "What did you do?" He said, "I dialed that number." Astonished I questioned, "Who replied?" He said, "The line was busy." We all laughed. Yes, our phone lines are often occupied, but God's is not. In the name of Jesus, we have access to the throne of God 24/7. He says, "Ask and you shall receive." Need to talk to Him today? *Just call He will answer.*

OUR OWN VOICE

It is a sad fact of our nature, a psychological fact, that our own desires can be so loud that they sound like divine commands. Shout long enough about what we want to do, and the echo will come back sooner or later, but it is our own voice, not the voice of God. People talk of how they wrestled with God over a decision, looked at it honestly, and had to admit it's an unenviable procedure. Is God like that? Hardly! In fact, they are wrestling with their own will, not God's. They want Him to agree. Do we really imagine we must wrestle with God to pry a secret out of Him about what He wants us to do? Surely, He would just tell us without an all-out wrestling match.

THE NAME OF JESUS OPENS THE DOOR

In the Old Testament, people called on the name of the Lord, but did not pray in His name. They presented themselves to God through faith in His promises. However, for New Testament believers, Jesus taught that in His name we have immediate favor. We get VIP treatment. The name of Jesus opens the door. God hears us. That is how we must pray, trusting in the grace of Christ. Your name represents an imperfect person, but if you come in Christ's name, the angels stand aside while you enter the throne room. You are righteous and holy, and God finds no fault. In Christ, you wear a seamless robe of purity and holiness. It never stains, never tears, never grows shabby, but you are robed fit for the presence of the King always, every day.

FAITH FOR TODAY

The way that Jesus speaks of prayer is not quite like some suppose. He said, "Ask, and it will be given to you... seek... knock..." (Matt 7:7). These words are in the Greek present indicative — be asking, be seeking, be knocking. But elsewhere He used a different tense (aorist) indicating a single, completed action — "Give us this day our daily bread." (Matt 6:11) Ask not once, but every day, "Give us this day." Ask for each day's need. That is how God likes it, not "having faith" for everything for a whole year, but coming to Him as children over and over, asking for the bread of life, and the Holy Spirit, daily, not once forever. We always receive every day.

CUTTING THROUGH LIKE LASER

In the darkness of a bedeviled world, our prayers cut the darkness like lasers, becoming channels through which God's blessing may reach earth, and transmitting the power-currents of Calvary and the Resurrection. Intercession jams the wavelengths of the devil. Certainly, the devil will resist, and the world will howl in protest, too long undisturbed. The works of Satan are many, but they must go. For this purpose, the Son of God was manifested, that He might destroy the works of the devil. (1 Jn 3:8)

Church/
God's
Family

UNLIKENESS OF THE BODY

A *body depends* on the UNLIKENESS of its members to properly function. (Eph 4:11) The modern world tends to de-personalize us and reduce us to a few types. If Christians are not different, the Holy Spirit would make them different. A body needs eyes, ears, feet, hands, each member unlike one another, so does the body of Christ. The world says that differences tend to fragmentation. Paul speaks not of strength through uniformity, but strength through diversity. We are all originals.

NO SOLO-CHRISTIANS

To *say*, "I want to be a Christian, but I don't want to belong to a church" would be like saying, "I want to be married but stay single!" You simply cannot become a Christian on your own. By new birth you have entered the family of God and belong to the "household of faith." (Gal 6:10) It means belonging to a group of people, rather than to an institution. Just as Jesus surrounded himself with the twelve disciples, we need to be with other followers of Jesus. The church shows us that the Christian faith is a "together" faith. When you became a Christian, you were not only brought into a relationship with God, you were brought into a relationship with other people, too. You became a part of God's people, the church, living on earth.

THE CHURCH THAT DOES NOT SEEK THE LOST, IS LOST ITSELF

The church is a lifeboat, not a pleasure boat. From the captain to the cook it needs all hands-on deck for soul-saving. The church that does not seek the lost is "lost" itself. Some excuse themselves by saying that in today's pluralistic societies the Christian half can never penetrate the other half. Why not? That is not God's idea or command. When He spoke through Isaiah He said: "When the enemy comes in like a flood, the Spirit of the LORD will lift up a standard against him." (Is 59:19) The standard of the cross will always be lifted against the enemy. Our job is to preach the cross and Christ crucified. The voice of God is as clear today as it was on the day when Jesus spoke to the eleven and said, "Go into all the world and preach the gospel to every creature." (Mk 16:15)

THE GOSPEL OFFERS LIFE

When a drowning dog is saved, it's pulled out of the water and dumped on the grass. But when Jesus saves people, it's quite different. The gospel offers more than a life-belt, it offers *life!* After having been rescued you are not left to yourself. The Good Samaritan (evangelist) picks you up and takes you to an Inn (church) where you will be loved and nursed.

RIVALRIES RUINED REVIVALS

The past holds tragedies. When doors opened, jealousy found Christian workers guarding their monopoly like diggers their goldrush stakeout. Rivalries sometimes ruined revivals. The harvest must not go unreaped while reapers merely defend their patches. Christ did not die to give people a career but to save the lost.

CANTEEN FOR WORKERS

The church is not a restaurant for spiritual gourmets, cultivating a discerning taste for food from the pulpit. It is a canteen for workers. When every Christian is a worker all strife stops. A pulling horse never kicks.

BROKEN PEOPLE

Churches are for broken people who need all the nursing and support available, and the laying-on of compassionate hands to heal the delirium of sin, not tongue-lashing and exclusion. John put an arm around shattered Peter after his lying and cursing denial of Jesus, took him to his home, saving Peter, who became — well you know. "He that comes to me I will never cast out," Jesus said in John 6:37.

Authority

AUTHORITY

Let's talk about authority. Thumping and shouting do not create authority. I have no objection to signs of life! But authority is a hidden secret within our own hearts. We dare to make authoritative utterances because we are deeply convinced of their truth. This is not dogmatism but reliance upon the Holy Spirit to convince our hearers. Authority rests on faith in the Word of God and the conscious awareness of His Spirit within us.

DOING THE WORD

Everybody in the Church accepts that we must continue what Jesus began teaching, but we cannot just teach and omit what He did. We must heal as well as teach. If we don't then there is no real continuation of Christ's ministry. We have only completed half the task, "Go and make disciples ... teaching them to obey everything I have commanded you." (Matt. 28:19-20) We have not a hair's breadth of a warrant for splitting His teaching from His healing. They are mutually supportive. He taught by what He did and said, "If I do not do the works of my Father, do not believe me." (Jn 10:37) NKJV The authority of His teaching rested on His miracles and His miracles on His teaching. If we teach what He taught, we shall do what He did, or our teaching becomes academic only. Jesus said, "[You] will do even greater things than these, because I am going to the Father." (Jn 14:12) Jesus spent half His time healing. To see His death as termination of that ministry is simply no credit to a changeless Christ. That is how the church becomes the manifestation of Christ again in a needy world. His compassion flows through our hearts and is seen in our eyes. It moves our feet as it moved His. Our hands become His hands and our voice His voice. Our arms of love are the only arms He must use on earth. We can do nothing without Him and He will do nothing without us.

FOOLPROOF RECIPE

This is how my parable begins. Let me call him John. John had a double story house, five-plus-five rooms. One day there was a gentle knock on the front door. When John opened, it was the Lord Jesus. "Please come in," John pleaded, "I will give you the best room in my house — it is upstairs." Well, Jesus is a gentleman and said, "thank you." The next morning someone hammered against the front door. When John opened it who was there? The devil. "No" shouted John, "I don't want you here" But the devil said, "I'm already in"— and a big fight started. Satan poured filthy temptation over him, it was horrible. By the evening John somehow got the victory and threw the devil out. Then he said, "wait a minute." I gave Jesus the best room in the house, why didn't He come to my rescue?" Jesus said to John "Look, you gave me one of the ten rooms..." John was on his knees and said "I can see my mistake. Sorry, Lord. Let's make 50/50." Jesus is a gentleman and accepted. The next day was a repeat of the day before. Somehow the devil got in and out and John was totally exhausted. "Why didn't Jesus come to my rescue today? I need to go and ask." The Lord said, "My son, why don't you give me all 10 rooms and then, instead of me staying with you, you stay with me?" John broke down. He pulled the key of the front-door from his pocket and handed it to Jesus. Now, he had given it all. The next morning, it was still dark, when someone was knocking at the front door so hard that the whole building shook. John jumped frightened and shaken out of bed crying "O, it's the devil again", when suddenly he heard footsteps — but this time inside the house. Jesus was marching in majesty and power towards the front door. He had the key. It now was His duty to answer the door. John was wondering what would happen and stood right behind Jesus when the Lord opened the door wide. Who was it? The devil of course. But when the devil saw Jesus standing in the door, he bowed low, very low indeed, and said "Sorry Sir, I knocked on the wrong door!" Some have given nine rooms to Jesus and on the door of room number ten they have written "Strictly Private." It is there where they have their secret sins and live their double life. But Jesus cannot be cheated. C'mon. Let's sing it together from the bottom of our hearts "All to Jesus I surrender, unto Him I freely give... I surrender *all*, unto thee my God and Savior, I surrender All."[5] This is my foolproof recipe.

TURNING ON THE LION

Samson met a lion on his way to Timnah (Jud 14:5-6). The man of God did not flee because something happened the lion knew nothing about, "...the Spirit of the Lord came mightily upon him..." Chasing fleeing victims gives lions an appetite for breakfast. But this man turned on the lion. The ferocious beast found itself facing a ferocious man. Snarling over his shoulder, the lion tried to slink off, but it was too late. Mighty hands lifted him. Samson, with his bare hands, "tore the lion apart as one would have torn apart a young goat." The church was never constructed for defensive purposes. The gates of hell should be invaded, not avoided. Offense is the best defense. Instead of waiting to ward off the devil's onslaught, turn the tide of battle and launch an invasion of the devil's territory.

FINGERPRINTS OF JESUS

Those who have been touched by Jesus Christ carry His fingerprints. His fingerprints are His miracles. You may have to look very closely, but you'll find them. Jesus touches spirit, soul, and body and sets the captives free. "Let the redeemed of the Lord say so!" (Ps 107:2)

"HE HAS HELPED ME"

When Jesus hung on the cross the Pharisees mocked him, saying, "He has helped others, but He cannot help himself." Many onlookers nodded their heads and said to themselves "Yes, this Jesus helped me too. Once I was blind but now I can see." "And I was in the dungeon of despair when this Jesus helped me," someone else nodded. Today Jesus is passing your way. Let others mock, but you put your trust in the Lord and receive your miracle.

HOLD YOUR GROUND!

Whilst Nehemiah was restoring Jerusalem, he was urged to hide from his enemies. I like his reply, "Should such a man as I flee? I will not...!" (Neh 6:11) Are the blood-bought people of God to surrender to bluster and threats? We are not given "...a spirit of fear, but of power and of love and of a sound mind." (2 Tim 1:7) Should such a people as we are, flee? Never! Hold your ground in the name of Jesus.

LIVING PEOPLE SHOW UP

The church in the Acts of the Apostles demonstrated that Jesus is alive. The proof should be in the church itself — its energy, love, and life. Well I am alive. I don't know of any book being written, or any lecture delivered, or anybody whatever that argues and tried to prove that I am alive. Why? Because living people tend to show up! All Jesus wants is a chance to show He is alive in the church. When the Church spends its time trying to prove Jesus was resurrected, naturally people think, "If Jesus is alive why do they have to spend so much effort and reason proving it?" It will be obvious.

DISCOVER THE RIVER

Some Christians are always "in the wilderness." They sigh deeply and say, "I'm going through another wilderness experience." The Christian who is not in the river of the Holy Spirit is out of his element. He's like the proverbial fish out of water. We are not called to be desert dwellers, like the people of Israel were for forty years, even though the Lord had promised them a land of rivers. Christ has promised believers rivers, not as a rare exception, but as part of their natural environment. We are not to be bank sitters, admirers of the passing waters, but river men instead. Jump in!

GOD'S BANNERS OF LOVE FLUTTER

This is God's world. Walk through it. The banners of His love flutter everywhere. The God who produced it is no turn-off — except to the prejudiced. Jesus came, typical of God, who designed the wonders of heaven and earth. He delighted those who met Him. They began to live — even the dead!

SHOT INTO THE HEATHEN HEART

The Apostle Paul was the burning arrow God shot into the heathen heart of the city of Rome. He did it from deep inside the city, from prison, and wounded the very center of paganism. Today we are at the frontline of spreading the gospel — you and me. We are not daredevils but dare-disciples and go in the name of Jesus.

MY HOME

The will of God is my home. I dwell in it. Though I travel the whole world to preach the gospel, I never leave home.

SATAN'S BRUISED HEAD

At Calvary Christ had bruised Satan's head. Hades opened its black jaws to devour another victim, then, too late, discovered, He was the Prince of Life. His lightning flashed into the gloom of the infernal caverns. His glory shattered the reign of the King of Terrors. Jesus stormed out again in resurrection power, leading captivity captive. The head of the serpent and the gates of hell were shattered. *Jesus Christ is Lord*

DANGEROUSLY CAPTIVATING

Was Jesus Christ boring? Well, He was national news. When Pilate handed Christ over to a death squad it wasn't for spreading gloom and hopelessness. Jesus was too dangerously fascinating and created too much excitement. "All the world has gone out after Him," said His jealous enemies. But, "The common people heard Him gladly." Police came to capture Him but were captivated by Him. They explained "Nobody ever talked like this man." This is Jesus, our Jesus!

JUST OPEN THE CAGE

When I see how Satan torments people with drugs and drinks and a host of unmentionable addictions, I cannot purr like a kitten, but want to roar like a lion for the whole world to hear: *Jesus Saves,* Jesus Christ is "the Lion of the Tribe of Judah" and has triumphed (Rev. 5:5). You don't need to defend a lion. Just open its cage. He knows how to prevail.

WHEN GOD SAYS, "I WILL"

When God says, "I will…" nobody can resist Him any more than a fly can resist a hurricane. It's wise to move along with the Lord. God's chariot is rolling. He says, "In the last days *I will* pour out of my Spirit on all flesh." (Acts 2) We either get on board or are crushed beneath its juggernaut wheels. Let's move with God. Let's move with the mover!

THE EXTRAORDINARY IS SO COMMON THAT IT IS ORDINARY

God plans for nothing to be ordinary. Jesus pointed to the lilies as examples of superb beauty — they were probably hyacinths, every petal and leaf of utter perfection. In the Kingdom of God, the extraordinary is so common that it is ordinary. Each person is special. The Shepherd with a hundred sheep searches for one gone astray. The boy David, the young outsider in Jesse's warrior family, was chosen to be anointed as the future King. Christianity is the religion of the unwanted. Faith is fertile ground in which God grows His plants and trees. He plants qualities in the man or woman of faith, which presently become admired anywhere. Little people take on stature by faith in Christ.

CHRISTIANITY IS NOT STOICISM

Christianity is not stoicism: we do not need endurance to get power, but power to get endurance. "Strengthened with all power according to His glorious might so that you may have great endurance and patience." (Col 1:11) Receive it. In the name of Jesus.

Miracles

CHANGING CONDITIONS

I grew up at the mouth of the River Elbe in Germany. When the tide was out, we boys played around the barges which were stuck in the mud. In my mind they were impossible to shift or move. But then the tide with the water returned. A missing element had come and there was a difference. The barges floated. I could even move them with my foot. When we preach the gospel, the tide comes in. The immovable becomes moveable, the incurable curable and the impossible possible. Praise God!

REPOSITIONING THE LOCALITY OF A FEW ATOMS

In the middle of Lake Galilee, the disciples suddenly saw Jesus. He was like a ghost emerging out of the gloom and spray. It was unbelievable — He was walking, treading the waves under his feet like snarling animals. He came right across to the boat and got in. Then, another inexplicable experience, for "immediately the boat was at the land where they were going." (Jn 6:21) It was all real but seemed unreal. The disciples never forgot it, could never fathom it, but took it as normal when Jesus was around. It goes without saying that the God who created the universe should know how to handle all things in a storm — who else? Well, Jesus showed He did. So, who is He? Need we ask? The answer is in John 1:1-2, "In the beginning was the Word. All things were made by Him and nothing without Him." Getting a boat across to shore in a moment of time should be no problem to the one called "the Word." It only takes Him to reposition the locality of a few atoms. Our God specializes in things impossible.

"WHERE ARE ALL THE WONDERS?"

God enables us to do the extra special because He looks for us to do miracles. Normally we all look to Him, sitting back and waiting for Him to perform. But He does nothing without us. Look at Gideon. He demanded of God "Where are all the mighty wonders?" (Judges 6) God's reply was to send Gideon to produce them! God wanted Gideon to display God's wonders. Today he waits for us.

HOW DOES A MIRACLE WORK?

How does a MIRACLE work? A friend of mine went for pipe-organ lessons but was astonished when the instructor told him to bring an overall on the first day. "An overall," he puzzled. "What has that to do with playing a pipe-organ?" Arriving for his first lesson the music master was waiting and said "Put your overall on. I am taking you inside this instrument. I want to show you what happens inside behind the consoles when you play outside." If we want a miracle, we should understand its inner workings. Come on, put your overall on — dive into the Word of God, and find out the how and why of God's wonders.

Healing

THE PATIENCE OF JOB

James speaks about the patience of Job. In what way was Job patient? Many have said that he was patient with his sufferings. The third chapter of Job in no way sounds like that. It begins "After this opened Job his mouth and cursed his day. Job spoke and said, "Let the day perish wherein I was born and night in which it was said there is a man child conceived." He continues in this strain for 26 verses in which one thing is very prominently missing — any sign of patience with suffering. In fact, the Bible does not display marked toleration of suffering. Unlike all other religions which demand resignation, Bible faith protests illnesses and pains. In the first five books of the New Testament, that is more than half of it, Jesus leads an attack upon physical suffering as the work of the devil. Christ displayed no patience with the world's misery. Job's patience was not with his afflictions but with God. This great man showed not a flicker of mistrust in that direction. Puzzlement yes, questions yes, frustration yes, but not agitated criticism of God. He uses some of the greatest phrases we know. "When he has tried me, I shall come forth as gold." "Let come on me what will. Though He slay me, yet will I trust Him." "I know that my Redeemer lives and though worms destroy my body yet in my flesh shall I see God." (23:10, 13:13 and 15, 19:25) The Lord later spoke saying that Job had spoken the thing that is right of Him. (42:7)

PEACE DEFIES HUMAN UNDERSTANDING

Peace springs from love and joy. It is their product. That's why Jesus could talk of "my peace I give unto you" on his very way to the cross. This peace is exclusively a Christian grace. It is driving, urgent and missionary. Peace is health (shalom) — to a Jew it is the same word. Peace is the absence of stress. It is full occupation of our mind and strength in fulfillment of life's destiny. Peace is inner quietness in the face of adverse circumstances. It defies human understanding (Phil 4:7).

FAITH IS NOT BUILT ON REASON

Faith is not built on reason or even on one's own personal experience of healing or the lack of it, but on looking to Jesus. A thousand years before Christ's incarnation a Psalmist wrote, "It is time for you to act, O Lord." (Ps 119:126) And 2000 years after Christ's incarnation that same Jesus is still "acting," working, as He did when He walked this earth. It is time for us to acknowledge it. "Take up your bed and walk," (Jn 5:8) Jesus said.

GIFTS COME WITH OPPORTUNITY

They are issued to workers as they clock in at the door. Like modern technology, God's work needs specialized equipment, but it is found "on the job." He does not hand it to us to keep handy in case we can use it sometime somewhere. The need of the healing gift arises when we are moved by the plight of sufferers. That is when the gift operates. Jesus was moved with compassion. The word means physically churned up and shocked. When your stomach turns over and you have to blink tears away at the sight of people, miserable and depressed with afflictions and ailments, and you feel like screaming in protest at their condition — go ahead, God will give all you need.

GOD'S THINKING

God is the "God of all comfort," not the God of all explanations. He did not come to tell us why, but how. When the leprous general Naaman came to Elisha for healing, the prophet sent a servant to tell him to go and wash in Jordan (2 Kings 5). Naaman was outraged. He said, "I thought he would come out to me, stand and strike his hand over the place." He thought, but the Lord didn't do it the way he thought. The gospel itself is God's thought, which to human thinking is foolishness — yet it is the wisdom and cure of God. Follow His Word and you will be comforted.

MIRACLES PERVADE

A woman was healed from what is called "an issue of blood." (Lk 8:43-44) The whole point is that Jesus took no action whatever. She got near to Him, touched no more than a portion on the edge of his clothing and instantly was healed. She had found the secret. Power and healing pervade the presence of Jesus. To be healed needs no special techniques or spiritual gymnastics. That is seen in Mark 6:56, "They laid the sick in the streets that they might touch if it were by the border of his garment and many as touched him were made perfectly whole." None of them was a religious athlete. They just got near to Him. There is healing in His presence. Jesus is passing your way today. Touch Him too.

JESUS LED THE CHARGE AGAINST THE DEVIL

Healing is a window into the heart of the Bible-God. He is not a remote and indescribable being who does nothing and lets everything slide. Among world religions that is exactly what Christianity does NOT say. Jesus never suggested that we bow to suffering as the inevitable will of God. Jesus had no track with fate (kismet), nor with re-incarnation (karma), obliteration (nirvana) and un-weeping eyes (stoicism). Christianity doesn't deal in theories but in power. His servants have no guaranteed magical omnipotence, but Christ is in action against everything that spells death, like sin and sickness, either instant or distant. When Jesus came into this world, he led the charge against all the works of the devil.

IF WE ONLY BELIEVED WHAT WE SAW, WHAT WOULD A BLIND MAN BELIEVE?

Physical optics are not the instruments to perceive God. He is a Spirit. Mortal eyes are too weak to discern the invisible God, the King eternal, immortal, invisible (Col 1:15 and 1 Tim 1:17). We must deal with Him as He is. "He who comes to God must believe that He is, and that He is a rewarder of those who diligently seek him." (Heb 11:6) But there is a better way of seeing. Eyes can play tricks. Plato the greatest of the Greek Philosophers said that nothing is ever actually how it looks to us. But Moses endured as seeing Him who is invisible. (Heb 11:27) If we only believed what we saw, what would a blind man believe? Radio waves fill your room but who would know without a receiver? One of God's great Bible names is the Lord is there. God is invisible Spirit, and that is that. It is as useless arguing and expecting God to be what He is not. Jesus said, "Blessed are those who have not seen and yet have believed." (Jn 20:29) They are on the track of truth — God is like that if we are to know Him.

DOUBLE BREAKTHROUGH

Four men had a literal 'breakthrough' of faith. Luke 5:17-26 describes Christ in a house crowded with Pharisees and teachers of the law, who had come out of every town of Galilee, Judea, and Jerusalem. Obviously, many of them had physical troubles, and the power of the Lord was present to heal them. But none of these religious people were healed. Then, four men brought a paralyzed man on a stretcher, and because they could not get through the crowd, they went up the outside stairs of the flat-roofed house, pulled apart the light coverings, and lowered the man down right in front of Jesus. Seeing their faith, he restored this man to health. It was a double breakthrough. They broke through the roof, and they broke through the unbelief of the crowd, which had kept them back from Christ. That happens every time somebody is healed. It breaks through the crust of unbelief of the world. It must; otherwise we will never get near Jesus at all. Believe God! It will please some people, and amaze everybody else.

COMPOUNDED OF LOVE

God is love. All His works are acts of love. So, five times in Matthew we read Jesus had compassion upon people. It didn't even need to say it. He was compounded of love and love was

His primary motive. However, His miracles were also to confirm His Word. He Himself spoke of them like that. He preached the Kingdom of God and healed the sick — it was all one message. It still is. Believe and receive it.

HEALING BREAD

Jesus met a non-Jewish widow outside of Israel in Sidon who asked Him for help and healing of her daughter. (Mk 7:24-31) Jesus tested her, speaking of "dogs"— She continued, and He replied, "Let the children be filled first, for it is not good to take the children's bread and throw it to the little dogs." Jesus describes people with RIGHTS and those without RIGHTS. "The Children" were ISRAEL and their promises and covenant. "The dogs" were outside the commonwealth of Israel. To Children: Bread is a RIGHT, a birthright! To outsiders: Bread is a GIFT, "tossed" as a favor! The woman saw: What was not hers by right, could be hers by GIFT, (favor/grace). She replied: Then let some crumbs of Israel's healing bread be tossed to those of us whom they call *dogs*. Jesus marveled at her faith and healed her daughter. It was said: If you want healing, first get saved! This is right and wrong: The Saved are under *promises* of healing. The Unsaved are under "gifts of healings." It rests on the graciousness of God! So, or so, we are safe in the arms of Jesus.

CLOSING CHURCHES AND HOSPITALS?

Closing churches? Ignoring the gospel? What are the consequences? Well, for one thing we are told that crime has increased 1,000 percent within one generation, but, for example, closing hospitals doesn't prove that the country is healthy. We urgently need God to save and heal our sons and daughters. We must preach the gospel by breaking the Bread of Life into edible pieces. *Jesus saves.*

BECAUSE OF LOVE

I don't play the piano to prove that I have fingers. Yes, of course, I have fingers, but I play the piano because I love music. Jesus doesn't set the captives free and heal the sick to prove anything. *He does it because He loves us.* Christ's coming brought the world a new springtime, new beginnings. The supernatural naturally produced miracles, as sunshine brings out the crocuses in spring. But crocuses are not why we believe in the sun, and miracles are not why we believe in Christ. It is the other way around — we believe in miracles because we believe in Jesus, who is the greatest of all miracles.

God

THE RIVER OF GOD IS EVER COMING

God is NOT a will be, could be or might be God. What He will be *He is now* and *Always has been.* "For I am the Lord, I do NOT change." (Mal 3:6) But it is different for everyone. "I am the Alpha and the Omega," says the Lord God, "who is, and who was, and who is to come, the Almighty." (Rev 1:8) Suppose you stand at a river's edge. You are at the river, yet also the river keeps coming toward you. The water we stand in will be the same water someone else will stand in tomorrow or downstream. *God is like that. He is here — and He keeps coming towards us.* "who is, and who was, and who is to come, the Almighty." The God of Moses and Elijah *is not behind us, but ahead of us.* It would be impossible and foolish for us to want to update the *eternal and almighty.*

REFLECTING LOVE

Our love reflects God's love, like the mighty sun reflects in a pocket mirror of a little boy. "We love Him because He first loved us." (1 Jn 4:19) Witnessing is one of the ways in which we express God's love. But no wife says, "I have made a commitment to talk about my husband." She just does it. Jeremiah said, "If I say, 'I will not mention him or speak any more in his name', his word is in my heart like a fire, a fire shut up in my bones." (Jer 20:9) To him, prophecy was not a well-considered decision but a burning necessity. That is the Lord God, the Jesus we preach. Our gospel is not made up of mysterious teachings issued by some guru in a cave. It is Jesus! Who else has arms extended to the unloved of the nations? Jesus... It is Jesus.

MINDLESS MATTER CANNOT MAKE MINDS

We are "made a little lower than the angels" (Heb 2:7), but only briefly, a very temporary "permanence." Even Job complains "My days are swifter than a weaver's shuttle." (Job 7:6) Yet there are some cheering facts about life. One is our make-up. We were not intended for short term; even our physical intricacies seem a waste for a mere 70-80 years, an over plus. But Ecclesiastes 3:11 says "He has put eternity in their hearts." We could not be what we are by coincidence, nor by a million, million accidental variations. The "Big Bang" did not generate intelligence and self-consciousness — we have intelligence enough to know that. Mindless matter cannot make minds. The answer is where answers to the riddles of life are all found — in Jesus Christ, the fountain of life, the One who calls Himself "the Resurrection and the Life." (Jn 11:25) He solves all riddles and answers all questions.

EMPTY TOMB — NOT EMPTY CHURCH

The Bible is a success story. It does not inspire us to fail. It inspires us to succeed. God has commanded us to advance on all fronts. The sign of a living Christ is the empty tomb, not an empty church. What is your vision? A god with His back to the wall? A god with a charitable cause? A god with servants living on next to nothing and calling it faith? a god with make-do churches, threadbare and struggling? What about Psalm 1:3, "Whatever he does shall prosper?" The first principle is to go for success. From Genesis to Revelation, God must be reckoned with by the kings of the earth. My God is the God who humbled mighty Pharaoh and caused Belshazzar's knees to knock and Felix to tremble. That disgusting emperor Nero had to hear the Word of God from the anointed and mighty Apostle Paul. Our God is omnipotent and not impotent. "For He alone is worthy!"

LOVE CANNOT HAVE REASONS

Love cannot have reasons. It is the ultimate. When God spoke to Israel, He said He had loved them for no reason. It was not because they were a great nation, for they were smaller even than the peoples to be driven out of Canaan. The Lord told them He loved them because of His love for them — which is no reason at all! The reason for love is love, which is God Himself (Deut. 7:7-8). Love is not God, but God is love.

GOD IS LIVING GLORY

God's glory distinguishes Him from all other gods, lords, and deities. Glory is God's essence, not gloom and darkness. Light attracts, and God draws us. Its reality is power, miracle energy, grace, truth, light, beauty and splendor. Blazing splendor identifies Him, awesome beauty, the mark of a peerless and living God. He challenges all the man-made gods and their wooden images saying, "To whom will you liken me and to whom am I equal?" (Is 40: 8 and 25, and 46:5) Like the sun is light, God is glory, but living glory. Whatever He touches is glorified. He made even the vandalized tree glorious when they nailed Jesus to it and the Tree, the Cross shines as our beacon in the godless night of this world. When Moses saw God's glory, his own face shone. When God comes, He comes in glory, and He enters our lives to fill us with glory — our lives and homes and future. No Christian home should be dull, lifeless but bursting with vitality, activity, joy, and richness.

GOD'S ANSWER IS CALVARY

Jesus was no more interested in philosophizing about illness than a surgeon is with a patient on the operating table. He offers no explanations. "The reason the Son of God appeared was to destroy the devil's work." (1 Jn 3:8, NIV) His answer is not words, but "by His stripes we are healed." God speaks, but His words are creative. He says, "Amen" to His own words and does what He says.

GOD LOCATED

For 2000 years God has been with us, located — even local. He does not sit in a nameless somewhere. He is not a diffused force conjured up with mantras, generated by meditation or concentrated by a pyramid-shape tent. He is here, geographical, news-reported! His set purpose is to bring us healing within, erase the conscience of guilt, and put our hand confidently in the hand of God. He counts no effort too great. His very veins were opened in His passion to save us, "tasting death for every man." Jesus is not religion, or theology, or doctrine. He is Him! The living Savior, the only Savior of humankind.

NO PASSING ACTION

We know God by His name, for it describes Him. (*Jahweh Rophi* — the Bible's proper name for God is *Jahweh, the Lord*, Ex 15:26). This is extremely important. His name does not mean some passing action — past or future. God does nothing incidental, and nothing out of character. His name is not about what He may do, but what He is, and what He does comes only from what He is, His name, for example, the God of healing is a permanent truth, His character eternally. Jesus saves because He is the Savior. Jesus heals because He is Yahweh Rophi. "Rise and be healed..."

ONLY VIA CALVARY

God's leading is always an event, never incidental, a casual stroll, but purposeful, day by day. By ourselves we just jog along hopefully, the best we can. Jeremiah 10:23 says "I know, O Lord, it is not for man to direct his steps." Jesus said, "Follow me!" Keeping an eye on life's changing interests, fashions, or ambitions, results in plowing a crooked furrow. It is bad and mad. God does guide, point to point, always positively, through all our days, and in all we do, our whole way of life. Let us be "fixing our eyes on Jesus, the author and perfecter of faith..." (Heb 12:2) He guides only via Calvary the fountain of life and cleansing.

THE ABSOLUTE ESSENCE
OF BIBLICAL FAITH

When Paul preached in Athens the locals said, "He seems to be advocating foreign gods." (Acts 17:18) But the apostles did not suggest a mere change of gods, i.e. Jesus instead of Diana. Jesus was not just a different, nicer god. To most Greeks, gods were just statues in the marketplace. People paid some homage to them and then forgot them. But the apostles were teaching nations about a God who had to be loved all day long and must never be forgotten. Christianity was a new way of life, not a few rites and ceremonies. Jesus was to be part of people's lives in a way the gods could never be. The problem is that it is far easier to perform a rite or two before some image and then get on with life in one's own way. That was the sin of Israel, who had often forsaken the Lord Himself. That is why the prophets said, "Remember the Lord" (see Neh. 4:14). The absolute essence of biblical faith was summed up in the one great commandment, "You shall love the LORD your God with all your heart, with all your soul, and with all your mind." (Matt. 22:37) NKJV

NOT JUST A COSMIC ENGINEER

God swings galactic systems into place, but he is not just a cosmic engineer. He is love. He loves people — with an intense passion. The Psalmist asks, "What is man that You are mindful of him, and the son of man that You visit him?" (Ps 8:4) Many understand that to mean that man is worth so little. But that is not what the Psalmist means. He was struck by the fact that God has contact with man. That changes the picture completely. If we judge man by his size or by his human limitations and weakness, he certainly does not amount to very much. But judge him by the fact that God concerns himself directly with his life and he suddenly acquires enormous stature. The One who orders all things according to His will gives us priority treatment. We are His VIPs! Imagine your president visited you. You'd be on the frontline of every newspaper the next day. God does not visit the moon or Mars or travel to stars at the edge of nothing; He turns towards you and me in love and says "Behold, I stand at the door and knock. If anyone hears My voice and opens the door, I will come in to him and dine with him, and he with Me." (Rev 3:20, NASB)

NO SHIFTING SHADOW

James says, "Every good gift ... comes down from the Father of lights, with whom there is no variation or shadow of turning." (Jas 1:17) NKJV As the NIV puts it, God "does not change like shifting shadows." The sun causes a shadow as it turns and the shadow moves. When there is no shadow, the sun is directly overhead at its zenith. God never casts a shadow at all, because He is always at the zenith. And He never shifts from that perfect position. The light of God is ceaseless, not temporary, and always fully radiant. His is the everlasting light that we are to eternally reflect. Our faces should not be veiled, as His glory will not pass away. We are being changed "from glory to glory." (2 Cor 3:18) — we are given more and more glory!

DIRECTION OF HISTORY

Politicians talk about the currents of history moving toward certain goals. Well, they are right about the currents of history, but not about the goals. God is working in the world to bring many sons to glory as Hebrews 2:10 assures us. When we give our lives to the great purpose of witnessing and evangelism, we will find that our lives are blessed with a deep satisfaction, and we will shine as the stars forever and ever (Dan 12:3).

AUTOMATIC AIR-INCREASE

The Bible speaks of the "proportion of faith" (Rom 12:6) — it is proportionate to the job at hand, index linked to the need. Like running and needing more air, your intake increases automatically. Size loses its meaning even for the task when it is a faith-task. The bigness of a hill, a house, or a molehill is all one to a bird flying over them. By faith "we shall mount up with wings like eagles." (Is 40:31)

ELECTRODE OF THE POWER OF GOD

Any doctrine or philosophy that doesn't lend itself as an electrode of the power of God is a waste of time. What difference would it make if some of our theological problems were solved? Would the right answers ever increase the degree of divine energy? Our mission is power, not routine. Our role is that of power people, laying the power lines into powerless lives. Winning arguments? I love to win souls.

GOD'S PRIORITY IS PEOPLE

As soon as we take an interest in witnessing and evangelism, God is interested in us. We become people after His own heart. There's more to God than making mountains and stars. His priority is people. He runs the whole universe with a saving objective. Our troubles trouble Him, and He calls us to share His concern. That is our Great Co-Mission.

PURE GOLD

Job said, "When he has tested me I shall come forth as gold." (Job 23,10) Testing does not make gold. Fire is not experimentation to create precious metal, it only smelts and releases it. The gold within Job would come forth as pure humanity, the image of His Maker. It is there, but in the state of ore. God means to get rid of the dross, the devil-stuff, the falsehood, the soul-trash. He wants us transparent as gold. God never gives up. He made man in His own image and likeness, but sin distorted it like a face reflected in disturbed water. Yet He perseveres. He'll recover that image, bring out the pure gold. We all have a glittering future. "It does not yet appear what we shall be." (1 Jn 3:2) "For those God foreknew he predestined to be conformed to the likeness of His Son." (Rom 8:29) Nothing could be greater than that.

WHO INVENTED JOY?

God invented joy — God, not comedians. God gave us the faculty to laugh — God, not the entertainment department. God gave us color and beauty — God, not the Impressionists. Being saved doesn't mean mustering up enough stamina for a twice-on-Sundays-in-church endurance test. No church-service would be an ordeal if Jesus led it. Monotony isn't a Divine invention. Something is wrong if worship is a yawn. We're in reverse gear. "Saved" people *love* — love God, people, God's Word, love worship, and love life.

RE-SHAPING LIVES

Jesus did not come just to talk, to persuade us to be good and decent. He never screamed condemnation on the wicked. He preached like nobody else ever did. His words are power words. Listen to them, receive them, and you go away with far more than good intentions. Jesus didn't preach to tell you to turn over a new leaf, but to turn you to a new life. In those days they talked about a potter working on clay and when it went wrong, he started all over again. In the Bible God spoke about people in His hands like a potter, re-shaping their lives. Nowadays we can work on more than clay. We recycle glass, metal, paper, oil. However, *we cannot recycle human nature.* With all our laws and police and armies, and psychologists, and educationalists we can't transform a murderer or habitual criminal, a drug abuser, a child molester, and turn him into a real gentleman, or saint. But Christ does. You can't unscramble eggs. No — but Jesus will give you a new one. God can put people back together again and does so every day. Christ's preaching was proclamation. It set things happening and they go on happening. We read that at creation God said, "Let there be Light" (Gen 1:3) and there was Light.

HANGING ON

My father went *fishing* and his *catch* was far different from what he or anybody else could ever expect — an incredible story. He was young, strong, and sportive. Out walking by the water one day he heard a cry for help. Looking across he saw a man struggling, in danger of perishing in the ice-cold water. How or why the man was there, didn't matter for my father. He was a strong swimmer and without a moment's hesitation, he jumped in the wintry flood, swam out to the man, grabbed him and saved his life. He brought the half-drowned victim to the water's edge and began pulling him ashore. But he felt a peculiar drag. Heaving the victim to safety seemed an unexpected weight, heavy work. He could not understand why. Then he saw why. To his astonishment, he found out what the dragging 'weight' was. Two more drowning people were hanging on to the first man's feet! He was saving not one man but three people. Three for the price of one! This can happen when we win just one soul for Jesus. Maybe it's a whole family. Rescue the perishing. Many "hang on" if we care to help one.

GOD'S ALPHABET

The name of Jesus spells everything. It is God's alphabet, from Alpha to Omega. We believe in Jesus. Dogmas and creeds are for our heads, but Jesus goes for the heart. He says, "I am the Way." (Jn 14:6)

WHY GOD CANNOT LIE

A friend of mine said, "If you wear a black shirt and I say it is white, I'm lying. But if you wear a black shirt and God says it is white, it then turns white." That's why God cannot lie. His Word and power are absolute. What about this, the Lord also says "Son, your sins are forgiven," or "rise up and walk," Let your faith kick in.

PERFECT UNITY

We might get a different picture of God from the Old to the New Testament unless we appreciate the eternal faithfulness of God. He may change tactics. He comes to people as they are and shows Himself against the background with which they are familiar, but the light of His love still gets through even when it is filtered through a glass darkly. The light that travels through clear air is the same light that radiates through a red sky, through dirty windows or through a prism. The light that came to Joshua was the same light that Moses saw in the burning bush and the same light the apostles saw on the day of Pentecost. It is the same light that Saul saw on the Damascus road and which Abraham saw as a smoking lamp. God's love may come as anger or as judgment, but it is still love. There is perfect unity between every revelation God makes about Himself in the Word. We may have to look for it, but it is there. That is why we constantly scan the Scriptures, to seek the Word's inner core, its unity, which is the unfailing unity of God.

Creation and Science

POSITIVE THINKING

Christian thinking is positive, but positive thinking is not always Christian. Negative thinking is never Christian, never Bible. The gospel itself is God's thought, which to human thinking is foolishness — yet it is the wisdom of God. By the Word we can have the mind of Christ. It challenges us to soar like the eagles to live in the dimension of faith.

GOD OPPOSES TYRANNY

We become what we were born to be only when we are "born-again" by faith in Christ Jesus. Christ said, "If the Son sets you free, you will be free indeed." (Jn 8:36) The world's greatest book on freedom is the Bible. The very idea of freedom came from the Bible, not from Greece or Rome. Read it! Remember God made the first free nation ever seen on earth, Israel, and He wants to put a sense of liberty in our very soul. God opposes tyranny. The gospel makes us the freeborn sons of God.

BOTH HANDS

"With weapons of righteousness in the right hand and in the left." (2 Cor. 6:7) Our right hand should be as righteous as the left hand. In other words, there should not be two sides to our character, but instead we should always be straight in our dealings and never devious. We should have more than an honest face. If that is the only honest part of us, we will soon be shame-faced.

ONE SINGLE GOD-DIRECTED DAY

Whatever we enter in our diary, God has the long-term operative calendar. "A day in your courts is better than a thousand." (Ps 84:10) His purposes rise above our priorities. We can be agitated, frustrated, impatient, but He knows where He wants us and when. We have our celebrations, birthdays, wedding days, but we can wait as God turns the pages of His appointment diary. One single God-directed day for us can affect the world more than 36,500 self-directed days, which comes out to roughly 100 years. Indeed, to God "One day is as a thousand years." (Ps 90:4) That is, a single day can be as effective as 1000 years when God makes it so. This is the God with whom we walk hand in hand on earth.

REPUTATION OR RENEWED LIVES

Zacchaeus worked for the occupying power of hated Rome and the people saw Jesus befriend him. It damaged Jesus' reputation. His foes would make much of it. His reply may have cut little ice with these resistant critics, but it uncovered the truth about the character of Jesus. He said, "The Son of Man came to seek and save what was lost." That sums up Jesus, our Lord. If it sums up any of us, it is enough that we are as our Lord. It is not reputation we seek, but renewed lives.

BLESSING RANK SINNERS

Jesus shocked religious leaders when He blessed rank sinners. The Pharisees considered them cursed, because they didn't know the law of Moses and religious traditions. Jesus befriended the sinful. He said, "The poor have the gospel preached to them." (Matt 11:5) That was a revolution. To the religious perfectionists the poor were untouchable, but Jesus preached to them, loved them, forgave, and healed them.

THE HEAVENS DECLARE THE GLORY OF GOD, AND HIS WORD ARTICULATES IT

That is the word we preach, the good news we share. There cannot be any other word; only one word can be true, just as existence can have only one reason and only one meaning. The unchangeable truth is that if the world does not relate to the gospel, it relates to nothing. The gospel explains it all and nothing else does. Disown the gospel and darkness falls. No other voice tells us what the world is for; no other light illuminates the mystery of our own presence on earth. Jesus says, "I am the light of the world. He who follows Me shall not walk in darkness but have the light of life." (Jn 8:12)

CREATION AND THE CREATOR

Creation relates only to the Creator. Nothing exists for itself; no one exists in isolation from others — except rebellious sinners, who then lose their only validity, which is God.

We are not our own meaning and without God we are irrelevant. Without God our world, its commerce, its hard-working activities, its governments and its institutions become vanity and vexation of spirit, as motiveless as the wind that blows from south to north and back again (see Ecc 1:6). "You are worthy, our Lord and God, to receive glory and honor and power; for you created all things, and by your will they were created and have their being." (Rev 4:11)

CROWN OR COFFIN

The crowning reward is in Christ. Whether we are "in Him," or we stay out. The choice is ours. We decide our destiny, either to die in our sins or die in Christ, to end either with a coffin or a crown, years of effort buried with us or translated into endless reward. "Be faithful to death, and I will give you a crown of life." (Rev. 2:10)

CREATION IS THE SIGNIATURE OF THE ALMIGHTY

Amid the wheeling galactic systems, the countless worlds like dust clouds, and the whole engulfing vortex, have we any significance? In this infinity can the weak voices of our proclamation of the cross register anything? What use is our gospel message against the vastness of such cosmic activity? There is no answer, except one, but that must be the true answer. "These are the things of God." He is their explanation, full and adequate. Creation is the signature of the Almighty. He formed and cast all visible things for Himself. The glory of the heavens is only a pale reflection of His glory. The burning nebulae are jewels that fell from His garments and scattered as He passed along. The Milky Way is a ring for His little finger. "By his breath the skies became fair and these are but the skirts of His ways," says Job. (Job 26:13) God created all things and told us why. He did not leave us guessing. His Word is greater than Creation for it exists by His Word. "O come let us adore Him..."[6]

THE REASON BEHIND THE UNIVERSE

Heaven and earth express His glory. Why did God make such an endless universe teeming with wonders? They are not made for our glory. God made them for Himself to express His glory, like a musician or artist in his music or paintings. "The heavens declare the glory of God." (Psalm 19:1) God made an immeasurable universe because He is immeasurable. He created it to show His own greatness and glory. To show us how great He is, He made the scale heaven and earth. Some have wondered, "Why those vast millions of great clusters of stars, whirling galaxies and awesome stellar systems?" Do we need such a big universe? Isn't it a wasteland of wonders? We are so egotistical we think that a thing is useless if it is no use to us. God happens to be important too — and He wanted living room. The Psalmist saw it and reminded us that, "The heavens declare the glory of God and the firmament shows His handiwork." (Psalm 19:1) That is what it is for, God expressing Himself and displaying His power. How could a God like we know make a small universe, be stingy and calculating? Why should he restrict Himself? How can a limitless God observe limits? He let loose His grand creative passions on a scale that bewilders us, trillions of suns, stars, and systems? God delights in greatness. And made an infinity universe to signify His own infinity. It characterizes His limitless power and lavishness.

God loves a cheerful giver. He is a giver on a scale that baffles our human science. It is time to realize that God needs a big universe even if we don't. Revelation 4:11 declares, "Thou art worthy, O Lord, to receive glory and honor and power, for thou hast created all things, and for thy pleasure they are and were created." It is to His glory.

CHRISTIAN STANDARDS

Human rights have been substituted for Christian standards. *Rights* represent only the personal views of a bench of judges of doubtful moral outlook. Their judgments have no ultimate sanction and are putting law and justice in jeopardy. The fear of God has evaporated. True progress is to know God. Science has no substitute for love. Adam and Eve were primitives but lived like kings walking with God. That is life as God intended it. God who created all things must have been an immensely wonderful friend. God has pushed hard for us to appreciate what He is and to understand His feelings toward us. The Son of God tracked across the universe to this one planet to introduce Himself — yes, He is that keen. "For God so loved the world that He gave His only begotten son, that whosoever believes in Him should not perish but have everlasting life." (Jn 3:16)

SCIENCE

It is time to tell the world that our universe is not a scientific universe, that the laws of science tell only one side of the story. The world was made for love, by love, founded on love for the pleasure of the Son of God. Truth cannot be expressed through mathematics any more than a human being can. Knowing how old I am, how much I weigh, and a few of my other vital statistics does not mean that you know me. The true me only flashes out from time to time in what I do. Truth is like that. One side of it may be examined by rational processes, in the laboratory or by chemistry and physics, but there's more to it. There is a nature in men and women which cannot be uncovered by the surgeon's scalpel. Our personalities respond to the power behind creation — *the love of God*. That is the way we are made and that is why the gospel impacts us profoundly. "Man does not live by bread alone, but by every word that comes from the mouth of God." (Matt 4:4)

"BIG BANG"

Talking of Creation. God enjoyed it, the Big Bang, spinning glittering galaxies into existence and stretching space to give room for their dance. He picked out one planet, Earth, tried His hand as a gardener and planted the Garden of Eden. There He introduced Eve to Adam, newly-weds in their first home. All this and heaven too! He laughed for joy, the pleasure of it, and it cost Him nothing... nothing, but... Salvation is God's greatest *work*. Look to Calvary. It cost Him everything, His Son, and left a wound in the heart of deity that never can heal. He was pierced for our sin.

STRATEGIC WEAPONRY

Christians have a world to reclaim and regain for God. The enemy has brought about vast destruction, death, and wickedness. Prayer opens God's armory with its superior weapons. If we think we do not need to pray, we do not know what we are up against. If we think we can manage on our own achievements, we simply make ourselves the devil's laughing stock. Prayerless means defenseless. Cleverness and science are a feather duster against a tank. The limitless greatness of the cross is needed against the cosmic evil.

TRUTH IN HARMONY

Gospel truth is in harmony and accord with the truth of creation. It is the God of creation who saves us because we are part of creation. He makes no distinctions between nature and spirit. He saves us where we are and what we are, covering the whole scene. The word of the gospel is physical-spiritual power. Unbelief shuts the door on God. Jesus saves *people*, people with feelings, physical and psychological. Jesus saves human beings of flesh and blood, not ghosts.

REDEMTION IS THE SECOND PHASE OF CREATION

We hear about evolution and revolution. But Christianity is regeneration and resurrection. The early Christians said they were a new creation. The Creator has started work again doing something greater. Redemption is the second phase of creation. "Therefore, if anyone is in Christ, he is a new creation; old things have passed away; behold, all things have become new. Now all things are of God..." (2 Cor 5:17 and 18a) A higher order than the human biological is coming into existence — we are the children of God, born from above.

WHAT MANNER OF LOVE

A man is not a good husband just by flexing his muscles. We could not be saved by brute force. In fact, no one knew what could save us. God committed Himself to the task, investing personal effort and sacrifice to the point of shedding blood. "Without the shedding of blood there is no forgiveness." (Heb 9:22) God was prepared for that at creation. It meant redemption. Creation was not cheap. Speaking a word was how he began it all, but it cost him tears, sweat, and later, blood. The six days spent making everything in creation culminated in six hours on a cross. "The Lamb was slain from the creation of the world." (Rev 13:8) Salvation is the artery through which the life-giving blood of all Scripture flows. When God made trees, He made one for his gallows. Christ was not a martyr but "the Lamb of God" to take away our sins.

GOD'S MIGHTY ARM

Christ clothed Himself with a material garment, His mighty arm, a human arm, sleeved in nature. When Jesus died on the cross the planet shuddered, and the sunlight flickered. The universe reacts to Him, for the whole natural order has met its Lord (Romans 8). However, that creation has been infected by evil. The Holy One took our nature upon Himself and suffered to be one with the world as it was. But its corruption did not corrupt Him. The world reeked like a slaughterhouse with the blood of murder and war, but the smell did not cling even to His robes. Then in His own body He experienced the horrors of sin and knew what it was like to stand in the shoes of the guilty — or rather hang on the cross of the guilty. What a wonderful, wonderful Jesus!

NEW ACCESS TO GOD

The coming of Christ was the beginning of the end for the devil. The spiritual advance goes on today. The armies of God form a new race of men and women, a holy nation, born again, presenting the Word of God with faith and prayer. We have new access to God, a new method of operation, and new authority, "by a new and living way," through Christ Jesus. (Hebrews 10:20) Victory is assured. "The creation itself also will be delivered from the bondage of corruption into the glorious liberty of the children of God ... For we were saved in this hope." (Rom 8:21 and 24)

HEROES OR LOSERS

All non-God operations are temporary, but the Jesus/ Holy Spirit partnership will swing past anything else that moves. This is part of God's order at creation and goes on forever — with or without us. We are free to be losers if we want — or heroes of faith. "Follow me..." said Jesus and it is the only right thing.

DEPOSITORIES OF ETERNAL LIFE

The power of God operates in two dimensions, in creation and in the church. These are God's two greatest works. He has put life into operation in the world. That life thrives in the world in a myriad of forms, from tall trees to great whales, from flowers and midges. Creation explodes with the life of God. It is set for a daily performance of divine omnipotence. The other area is in the church. It is His greater creation, brought into existence by the manifestation of resurrection and immortality. That is where His power is to be found. His glory and power reside in the people of God, the depositories of eternal life, and the energy retorts of the creative forces of God. We live in resurrection life. "The Spirit of him who raised Jesus from the dead is living in you. He who raised Christ from the dead will also give life to your mortal bodies through the Spirit who lives in you." (Rom 8:11)

Forgiveness/Christmas

WE ALL NEED FORGIVENESS

You can have forgiveness for your biggest sin; but you *need* forgiveness for your smallest sin. To God it does not matter if our sins are big or small, many or few. Our sins are no more a problem, because Jesus shed His precious blood for them and they will be forgiven and wiped out once we receive Him as our personal Savior. Just one thing matters... *We all need a Savior! We all need Jesus!*

ATONEMENT

God cannot forgive except by the atonement. It needs more than omnipotence or love. He did not just overlook our sin. It meant gathering up this evil and taking it into His own bosom like a fire. Sin necessitated Calvary. It finds its dreadful finality in Him. The music of God gained a *major* mode, while we are called upon to "Rejoice in the Lord always..."

CHEERFUL FORGIVER

The first advantage of a Christian is everybody loves a cheerful giver, and a cheerful forgiver. A Christian gives without remembering and receives without forgetting. For new creatures in Christ Jesus, getting becomes giving. Jesus heals the itchy palm and makes it allergic to filthy lucre. Covetousness becomes charitable. Zacchaeus, that heartless little extortioner, found new pleasure — compassion and charitable giving. Jesus doesn't like us holding too tight to our money. If our hands are full He can't give us more.

GOD REMEMBERS TO FORGET

If God forgives us, we must forgive ourselves. It is not for us to say that we cannot. God is the judge, not we. If He forgives, we dare not deny God's power. Who are we to condemn ourselves when the "Judge of all the Earth" acquits us? (Gen 18:25) The Bible says, "God is just and the justifier of him which believes in Jesus." (Rom 3:26) And that, "If we confess our sins, He is faithful and just to forgive our sins and to cleanse us from all unrighteousness." (1 Jn 1:9) We can stand before God as if we had never sinned, cleansed by the precious blood of Jesus Christ. Our sins, recorded in His mind, He "will remember no more." (Heb 8:12) God remembers to forget.

SAVING TRUTH AND FAITH

I know that we can find grains of gold in the sand. Elements of good may be found even in false faiths (see Rom. 1). But not all that is good *saves,* and not all truth is *saving truth.* Good advice and wise maxims won't bring forgiveness. Jesus didn't come to give us advice, dispense knowledge, or teach us to find our inner light. He came so that we might have *life* and have it more abundantly.

THERE IS ROOM AT THE CROSS

Look at the adulterous woman at the feet of Jesus in John 8:3. She is utterly broken. Then watch the Pharisees being hit by Holy Spirit conviction of their own sin. See how uncomfortable they become? They put in the reverse-gear and "...went out, one by one" (vs 9). I feel that this is one of the greatest tragedies in the Bible. Please allow me to say that I would have made a different move. If I had been there, being convicted of my own sin, I would *not* have stepped back but stepped *forward*. I would have knelt next to that woman. I would have lifted my hands and cried, "O Jesus, I have not committed adultery, but I've done so many other sins. Please forgive me, as you forgave her!" Over time many millions have knelt there and received forgiveness, total salvation. This moment you are one step away from the feet of Jesus. Look at Him, He beckons you. Please kneel at His feet! There is room for you as well — "there is room at the cross for you." Will you?

THE ULTIMATE GOOD

Sickness is not the ultimate evil; therefore, healings are not the ultimate good. Sin is the ultimate evil and forgiveness of sin the ultimate good. Yet Jesus does it all: He saves sinners and heals the sick — today.

JESUS ALWAYS CARES

Having faith in God means having faith in what God is and what He has always been. If He answers prayer once, we can rest assured that His natural response to prayer is to answer it. If He has ever cared for one person, it is because He always cares — for all. If He heals one suffering individual, it is because He is a healer; it's in His nature to heal. If He forgives one repentant person, it is because He is the forgiver. If He ever saved one human being, it is because He is God our Savior. The gospel reflects God's spontaneous dynamism.

NOT CLUBS FOR THE PERFECT

Churches are not clubs for the perfect. They are clinics for the sick, the wounded, and the maimed, where those a bit stronger help those who are still weak. The forgiven forgive. The healed heal. The comforted comfort others. Our role is not to kick people when they are down. They are the devil's victims, and rather than scorn we should pour on them the oil of understanding and bring recovery and joy.

END OF ALL BLOOD-FEUDS

Wicked men had bound Jesus lashed and crucified Him — the innocent One, unlawfully and unjustly. Should His death not be avenged? But Jesus did not cry out for vengeance. Instead He prayed, "Father, forgive them." (Lk 23:34) Whoever was guilty of Christ's death, they were forgiven by His prayer, whether they were Greek, Roman, or Jewish. The blood of Jesus, which they shed, was their redemption. Their pardon was handed to them at the very cross they erected. It was written by the pen of God dipped in the fountain of the precious blood of His Son. Instead of coming to avenge our sins, Jesus allowed all the vengeance due to us to fall on Him. Jesus offered His own blood to put an end to all blood feuds forever! "He himself is our peace, who has made the two one and has destroyed the barrier, the dividing wall of hostility. He came and preached peace to you who were far away and peace to those who were near." (Eph 2:14 and 17) That is *Jesus!*

"JOY TO THE WORLD..."

Jesus came. "Joy to the world, the Lord is come." Christmas Day. The date does not matter, or the Gospels would have told us. The heathen made some days very special for their heroes, festivals, and gods. But the coming of Christ has obliterated all such glory and remembrance. Every day is His. What is the fame of saints, gods, and great men compared to the glory of Christ? His day is acknowledged by nations that know little else about Him. If any day has been marked for any other, He hallows it, even the most notorious. The ancient Greeks kept up their wicked and blooded Dionysian traditions — but the name of Jesus has overcome all such calendar pollutions.

MERRY CHRISTMAS

To friends we send cards. To special friends we send gifts. But to the ones we really love we go personally. Praise God, that's why Jesus came personally. He was born in a manger. He really loves us. Aren't you glad? Merry Christmas.

CHRISTMAS ANGELS

Christmas decorations show angels as sweet little babies. "How cute!" But when the shepherds in Bethlehem saw the mighty angelic beings, they didn't giggle but "were greatly afraid." (Lk 2:9) The Bible says that those who saw angels were often frightened. Angels are described in various ways — at the tomb of Christ as two men in white (Acts 1:10), but on other occasions as awesome beings. John the Apostle was so impressed with an angel he wanted to worship him (Rev. 19:10). Daniel gives us a full description. He was overcome and was sick for three days. "Behold a certain man clothed in linen, whose loins were girded with fine gold of Uphaz: His body also was like the beryl, and his face as the appearance of lightning, and his eyes as lamps of fire, and his arms and his feet like in color to polished brass, and the voice of his words, like the voice of a multitude" (Dan 10:5). But read Revelation 20:1-3 "An angel laid hold of the dragon, that old serpent, which is the Devil and Satan, and bound him a thousand years, and cast him into the bottomless pit, and shut him up and put a seal upon him." That is the power of an angel. Merry Christmas!

SEE A GREAT LIGHT

At Christmas Jesus broke through the devil's darkness, as had been prophesied centuries before, "...the people that sat in darkness have seen a great light" (Matt 4:16 and Is 9:2). That light has shone ever since, and the darkness has never been able to put it out (Jn 1:5). Enjoy your Christmas.

CHRISTMAS ARGUMENTS

People ask, "Do you like Christmas?" Like it? God planned the world for it! That was the key of history locking together all days. Without Christmas the world would be meaningless. The Incarnation and work of Christ are God's greatest achievement. Not to worship on Christmas day is scandalous. It is *His* day, not the festival of fried geese. Those who quibble about the 25th of December being once a pagan mid-winter feast have no perspective whatever. They may as well say we can't grow wheat in a field because some thorns grew there before. "Beyond all question the mystery of godliness is great: He appeared in a body!" (1 Tim. 3:16)

CELEBRATING JESUS

Christmas is a festival like no other. No other religion has such a time as Christmas. What it celebrates is not a doctrine, or an obligatory observance, or traditional ritual. It is a spontaneous burst of hilarious joy coming from a revelation of the wonderful, glorious, God and Father of our Lord Jesus Christ. What a God He must be to be "the God and Father of Jesus!" (Rom 15:6) And what a Son He is! What a Savior! The Lord Jesus Christ is whatever we read of the Lord our God. "Be glad in the Lord and rejoice!" (Ps 32:11) Have a wonderful Christmas! You may as well — God wants you to have it.

CHRISTIANS ASTONISHED THE ROMANS

The Christians astonished the Roman world. Rome tried to destroy them, but they only multiplied. The Romans gloried in strength. The Christians gloried in their weakness. The Romans believed in hate and revenge. The Christian believed in love and forgiveness. The Romans believed in imperial authority, the Christians said, "Jesus Christ is Lord." The Romans believed in the sword. Christians said they would conquer the world with love. And they did.

THE PEN OF TRUTH

The gospel is not vague lovingness, fondness or Christian charity. The pen of truth is dipped in blood to write salvation from Calvary. We are not redeemed by the casual nod of an easy-going almighty God. The mouth of Jesus' gaping wounds speaks forgiveness and a welcome. The gospel rings with the cry from Eden, "Adam, where are you?" and with reverberations from Gethsemane and Golgotha too.

WE CANNOT CLEANSE OUR SOUL BY WASHING OUR FACE

Christianity is a sinners' religion. It has nothing for the perfect. They would have to start a new religion. As it says in Jeremiah 17:9, the human heart is "desperately wicked." We can't cure heart disease by wearing our best clothes. We can't cleanse our soul by washing our face. Respectability is only outward. To be a Christian starts with forgiveness. That is what we must preach. That is evangelism — to stress it, to hammer away at the need of it. "This day is the day of salvation."

EXCLUSIVE BRAND-NAME

Human ideas never yet plucked a guilty conscience from anybody's breast. Science forgives no sins; it is not saving knowledge. Salvation has only one exclusive brand name — *Jesus Christ the Lord*. Not Plato, Aristotle, Newton, Einstein, or one founder of the great eastern one religions was a savior, although the people certainly needed one. They had plenty of ideas, but only Jesus saves. "There is no other god like you, O Lord; you forgive the sins of your people..." (Mic 7:18)

Service/ Ministry For Jesus

PUSH THE BOAT

When Jesus wanted to preach He got in a ship and told His disciples to "push off a little from the land." (Lk 5:3) If we want the Lord to work, there must be human thrust. Let us get the gospel ship moving. Every revival has been like that — somebody not only prayed but also pushed the boat out and confronted men and women with the gospel. Jesus tells us to move today.

SERVICE SHAPED

Service as Jesus shaped it is always a partnership with Him. The Christian life is a joint servanthood — the only one, with Christ. Jesus changed the work ethic forever. He made service Godlike. (see 1 Cor 3:9)

UNALTERABLE CALLING

Peter was a man of action, but this virtue was also his failing — his impulse to act was too often unrestrained. He spoke when he shouldn't have. When he heard Jesus talk about being taken by His enemies, Peter played the big man, the hero, the protector of his Master (see Matt 16:21-22). Taking Jesus under your wing is quite an undertaking! Asking Jesus to put His trust in you, imagine that! That was Peter-then.

The true beginning of self-confidence is placing your confidence fully in Jesus. Lose confidence in Him and sooner or later your own boastings will burst and look as sorry as pricked balloons. When Jesus was arrested and tried, Peter was amazed to find himself shrinking. He became the shrinking man, so small that the words of a servant girl frightened him. So, he put on an act, pretending to be like every other man around. He warmed himself at a fire with other godless characters and became one of them, cursing and swearing, denying that he had anything to do with Jesus of Nazareth (see Matt 26:74 and Mark 14:54).

When Jesus first called Peter, He said, "Follow me" and gave him a marvelous catch of fish (see Matt 4:19). Then came three wonderful years with Christ, until the cross ended them. That brought Peter crashing down, a fall from great heights. Those marvelous days with Jesus seemed to vanish like a mirage. Peter just shrugged his shoulders and went back to square one, back to what he knew — fishing. That, however, was where Jesus had first stepped into his life and called him. And that was where Jesus stepped in again. Jesus met Peter fishing again — the same Jesus as yesterday, today, and forever. He worked the same miracle, a great catch of fish. And then Jesus again said the words He had said three years before, "Follow me!" (Jn 21:19) "For the gifts and calling of God are irrevocable" (Rom. 11:29) NKJV This is as true for you and me, as for any other child of God.

REJECTED REQUEST

In Luke 15:19 the Prodigal Son pleaded with his father "... make me one of your hired servants..." That is the only request the father rejected. He had many servants, but only two sons. The father wanted his son back. The difference between a servant and son is this, both work hard and for long hours, from morning till night. Only at night the dissimilarity becomes apparent. The servant goes and asks for his pay — the son does not. Why not the son? Because the son knows something the servant doesn't know. He knows that the day will come, when all that belongs to his father will belong to him. Do we serve Jesus Christ just as a servant — for instant reward, recognition, and pats on the shoulder? Or are we sons who know that an incorruptible and undefiled inheritance that does not fade away is reserved in heaven for us? (1Pet 1:3-5) Let us not be man-pleasers but God-pleasers.

FAITHFULNESS IN SERVICE

"He that receives a prophet in the name of a prophet shall receive a prophet's reward." (Matt 10:41) Christ did not say here "in my name," but "in the name of a prophet." That is, accepting a prophet as a prophet and helping him, brings an equal reward. Rank is abolished in Christ — it is faithfulness in service that counts, and one service does not outrank another. Christ washed His own servants' feet, an act for which no supernatural powers are needed.

AFRAID?

People ask if I am not afraid traveling the world all the time to preach the gospel. Well, most people die in bed, and yet we go back to bed every single night. So, "Underneath of us are His everlasting arms." That is enough for me and for us all. As Job said, "I know that my Redeemer lives." (Job 19:25)

PLATFORM OF THE WORD

Scripture is God-inspired to express God's concerns. What concerns Him should concern us. The world is a continuous swirl of human events, thoughts and reactions that God has been watching for thousands of years. "The Lord is on his heavenly throne. He observes the sons of men; his eyes examine them." (Ps 11:4) We may be unaware of God's fatherly gaze, but the Holy Spirit knows people and life's intricacies and how to touch the secret springs of human hearts — perhaps from surprising angles. To preach effectively, we must stand on the platform of the Word. Our divine instructions, like Timothy's, are to "preach the Word" (2 Tim 4:2) — not just a collection of commentaries on it!

LIVING IN THE SPIRIT

David knew that no stone he could sling would bring down that blaspheming thug, much less his shepherd's staff. He said he did not have a sword and yet declared he would cut Goliath's head off. True faith attempts what unbelief would never dare to tackle. That is a true work of faith when you can say like Paul, "I can do all things through Christ who strengthened me." (Phil 4:13) Too many Christians live on the level of the possible, the normal. The entire program of Christ is to lift us all to super-human levels. We become literally children of God, instead of children of men. We can live on the level of the supernatural instead of the natural. We live in the Spirit instead of the flesh. Paul said, "The life I now live I live by the faith of the Son of God who loved me and gave Himself for me." (Gal 2:20) That gives life, fullness, and quality and makes a man or a woman something they could never otherwise be.

TWO GREAT REVELATIONS

Two great revelations come to us through the Word — God is a consuming fire and God is love. They combine in a single flame of love. That image is central to an understanding of the Word and we cannot afford to neglect it. God originally revealed Himself to Moses as fire. It was a privileged moment in Moses' life, but Moses did not go off and spend the rest of his life merely talking about his experience. God commissioned Moses for a specific task and the fire leaped from the bush into his heart. That day he started out on the most extraordinary career any man would ever know, changing the future of the whole world. Whatever God reveals about Himself is meant to have a practical impact on our lives not simply to give us a topic of conversation. He does these things to put fire in our belly, not to given us an experience of euphoria, emotional satisfaction, or even blessings and thrills. Moses did not go back to the wilderness bush for a repeat experience. He went from there as God directed him. Then, 1,500 years later, on the day of Pentecost, the fire of God appeared again in Jerusalem where 120 disciples were sitting together in fellowship. It rested on each of them. Like Moses, they did not go back for a repeat experience. The fire had empowered them that day and they went out to do the job awaiting them.

FLAMBOYANT ACCESSORIES

We live and work and aspire like all mortals on the planet, eat and dress in fashion, enjoy the good things that men and women do like the worldlings. But we are *not* worldlings. The kind of clothes we wear is not a mark of our faith. Jesus said the Pharisees made long prayers in public and wore flamboyant religious accessories on their head or wrist. The children of God don't use such outward indications, such as their fashions, but walk the streets like any other person. They are clothed with humility and wear the garment of praise. Their difference is in themselves, identified with love, and faith, and their way of life, (see Rom 12:2). "Follow, follow, I will follow *Jesus*..."

JESUS AND THE ROMAN TAX-COLLECTOR

Men come and go. Myriads of stars appear, but sunrise eclipses them all. When *Jesus* appeared, the world was cowering under the iron wings of the Roman eagle, its imperial talons clawing the treasuries of nations. It is at a customs tax check point in a Roman backwater that we can get a typical glimpse of Jesus. The tax man sat in a single-room little office at the top of the street and had set his table clear of the hard sun slanting through the square doorway. Straggling toll-payers had called that morning. Levi usually kept them waiting, to impress them with how busy and important he was. Then another visitor blocked the light. Levi went on writing, his head bent over his accounts. Taxpayers awaiting his pleasure usually fiddled. Whoever this was now, however, stayed quiet. A full minute passed. Then a sense of being scrutinized began to disturb Levi's official composure. Still writing finally he snapped "Yes?" Silence! Annoyed, Levi with a sour glare looked up and met the eyes of Jesus Christ. He had seen Him before, but this was an experience, a true soul-encounter. Jesus was silent, smiling, not a formal social smile, but a smile that was an embrace, an overture, a personal gesture to Levi — a whole new episode. Confused with mixed reactions, for the moment the official was lost. Then startled he realized this man's hand was resting over his own on the table and leaning nearer, looking intently at him. Levi's pen left his fingers. How long the moment lasted Levi didn't know, but finally Jesus spoke. "Levi," He said, "Follow me!" That was all. Levi never knew why, but somehow the situation seemed full of an immediate importance. He got up, packed everything away, made the tax office safe and went out into the street following Jesus. He followed Him for the rest of his life. Levi died a martyr 30 or 40 years later. Jesus had come, not just into history, but into Levi's life, as if there was nobody else.

TOO SWEET?

Somebody said that I would follow Jesus "with too much devotion." But who can prove that my coffee is too sweet for me? It is a matter of personal preference. Not so? As for me, I cannot get enough of Jesus. "To me He is so wonderful — because He first loved me."

UNCLEAN LIPS DID NOT MATTER...

People speak of "the call of the prophet" in Isaiah Chapter Six. But he was never called. He volunteered. Isaiah overheard God say "Whom shall I send? And who will go for us" as if addressing another partner in the Godhead. He did not say, "Isaiah, will you go?" Isaiah realized God would send anybody willing. He ventured to offer himself. "Here I am. Send me." The Lord did not hesitate or ask Isaiah to submit his résumé first. He just said "Go!" Unclean lips did not matter. They were purged so that Isaiah's mighty voice was and is heard through millennia, "*Thus says the Lord.*" What a transformation in Isaiah.

FAILURE OF BELIEVERS

The failure of believers under the attacks of Satan is common. Some people sin openly and conceal their goodness. Others sin secretly while maintaining an appearing of goodness. Paul wrote, "Judge nothing before the appointed time." (1 Cor 4:5) We are not qualified to pre-empt the judgment of the all-wise, all-knowing God. Some men and women fight more temptations in a day than others do in a month. And big men can sin in a big way, a small fault becoming magnified through the lens of fame. But Jesus never failed nor fails — not even Peter when he denied his Lord. What a wonderful God.

SERVICE OR SHOW?

Exercising the gifts of the Spirit we can be like spiritual body-builders, developing for the sake of being strong. What is the use of a man being able to lift 300 pounds above his head on a show if he cannot lift a finger to help his wife in the kitchen? What is the use of all our outcry for power if we do not do the jobs that need to be done — the door to door evangelism for example, or Sunday school work? The release of the power of the Spirit is never possible while we are not active. When we apply ourselves to do the will of God in service, God sees it as us making ourselves ready. The same God who is behind the healing miracles is behind all the "activities," the willing service to God.

THE REAL THING

God wants His people to be matchless. They are redeemed, so let them say so. They are His workmanship, let them look like it. They are new creatures, let them act as such. We don't "put it on," to be artificially devout. We are to be "the real thing."

FROM PROPHECEY TO PROPHECEY

As a young man I went from prophecy to prophecy. Today I go from fulfillment to fulfillment. Now I fit Joel's category when he says, "Old men shall dream dreams..." (Joel 2:28 and Acts 2:17) God gives dreams, but they only come true when we wake up. Let's not dream all day. Let's rise and act.

TRIUMPHS OF FAITH

The Apostle Paul, this unknown Christian, a lone little Jew, found Europe and Asia full of fear — fear of spirits and omens, fear of their vengeful and moody gods, fear of the heavens above them and the depths beneath them, fear of the future, and fear of the mysterious world around them. Its millions bowed in spiritual darkness under a morbid dread of death. Paul's fear of God placed him on higher ground, and he said, "For to me, to live is Christ, and to die is gain" (Phil 1:21). These are the triumphs of faith!

A THISLE-HARVEST MAKES NO BREAD

The ordinary cares of life can become thistles, which smother the living seed of the Word of God. But a thistle harvest makes no bread. I want to give you a helping hand to plant your feet on higher ground and purposes — God's most wonderful eternal Kingdom.

JESUS' YOKE

Jesus said, "Take my yoke upon you." (Matt 11:29) He took our yoke, the yoke of rebellion, but we take His, the yoke of the divine will. He shares with us His sovereignty and the disposition of His activities. To govern the world, He relied upon people cooperating with Him, and praying. Prayer was arranged from the moment of creation to be part of His ongoing scheme. He planned to do nothing without our prayers and us. That is the way the world is, of which we are a part.

DISCIPLE MEANS "LEARNER"

Jesus was not a spiritual policeman. He did not discipline the disciples. That is not what disciple means. Disciple means "learner." He never ordered them about, interfered, or dictated in daily affairs. They came and went as and when they wished. It was all left to their wisdom and discretion. That is how Christ deals with us. Give Jesus our lives and He then makes them our own.

NO SACKCLOTH

One morning Jesus walked along the edge of Lake Galilee and beckoned to a few local fishermen. He said, "Follow me." (Matt 4:19) At that moment, everything began for them. "Everything" had only been fish, and then it became people, action, and changing world history, with ever-increasing faith, ever-increasing effects. Jesus did not call them, you, or me, to switch off our smiles and to wear sackcloth. It was not to turn people into religious fanatics. He was not so conventional Himself! The disciples caught His bubbling spirit, which challenged the stuffy establishment. He showed them new things, especially faith and love, and by them they conquered the world.

JESUS CALLS US "COME"

Above the roar of wind and the wash of waves the voice of Jesus is heard. When we are rendered speechless with dread, we hear Christ say "Come." Peter put one foot over the gunwale... then throwing doubts aside he dropped over the side, and... the waters under his feet held him, as stable as stone. *Jesus* had come! You can do the same and have the same experience. *Jesus* says *"come"* to everyone today in Matthew 11:28. Do it!

MERE HUMANS REPRESENTING GOD

One of the most wonderful things about God is His willingness to be represented by man. How can it be possible for a mere human being to represent Him, the Almighty, in any way at all? It certainly would not be possible by mere human effort or aspiration. It is not only by the will of God but also by the glorious fact that we receive the divine nature. We are born again of God and He is more than our recognized Father, for the Spirit bears witness that we are the children of God and His children bear His image.

WOMEN-PREACHERS

I was asked why I allowed women to preach the Gospel and replied, "If I as a man were drowning in a river, I wouldn't care if a woman or a man threw me a lifeline. Evangelism is an emergency-operation and we are all called to engage in it."

THE ROAD FLATTENS AS WE GO

I remember first travelling from Germany into Switzerland and came to the soaring barrier of a mountain. My little car seemed to tremble. I stood overwhelmed. Then I noticed a constant sparkle across the face of that imposing mass. Hundreds of vehicles tracking back and forth on the zigzag roads, slowly climbing up and up, conquering the steep heights till task accomplished. God declared "Every valley shall be raised up, and every mountain and hill made low; the rough ground shall become level." (Is 40:4) The road that looks steep ahead flattens as we travel. That is how life is as we depend on God.

OVER-FULFILLED

Jesus said to the woman at the well "go and call your husband." (Jn 4:16) It is not known if she brought her "husband," but she over-fulfilled her quota by bringing everybody else's husband. Her only message was *Jesus*. She could not debate about God; she knew nothing about Him. Debate is not our job. We are not religion pushers, church publicists, or spiritual insurance salesmen. Evangelism is not the hard sell but simply the good news of Jesus Christ. As in the case of that woman, Jesus saves sinners to save sinners. Let's go and tell our neighbors.

DON'T FOLLOW A PARKED CAR

Never follow a parked car; you will get nowhere. And never follow a parked pastor either. Keep following the move of the Holy Spirit.

PHANTOMS

Fear is forged in hell — issued by Satan as a standard weapon to all demons. They are full of fear themselves, like scorpions are full of poison. Satan wants to sting us — to make us all sick with fear and its paralyzing force. But: *fears are illusions, they are phantoms.* They will only take on substance if we accept them. God promises: "No weapon that is formed against you shall prosper." (Is 54:17)

NOT LOTS OF RULES

Jesus doesn't give you lots of rules. He keeps His hand on yours, and makes sure you keep on the path, you keep true, and you reach your destination. Jesus is the shepherd of the sheep — He doesn't tell you where to go, but He leads you. He doesn't send dogs barking to direct you. He doesn't sit in heaven shouting down criticisms of your life — He guides you Himself. Put your trust in Him — that is all you need to do. He said, "I will never leave you nor forsake you." "Come unto me all you who are weary and heavy laden, and I will give you rest. *Learn of me*, for I am meek and lowly in heart, and you shall find rest for your soul." (Matt 11:28) "It is well with my soul[3]..."

RAINBOW AND WAR-BOW

When Noah saw the earth desolated by the flood, he must have been traumatized. Afterwards, whenever the skies grew dark overhead, he would need assurance. God said, "I do set my bow in the cloud and it shall be a token of a covenant." The rainbow is the flag of God, the seven-colored royal standard. No icon, no regimental colors, no empire symbol could match that! The word "bow" in Genesis 9:13, is the same Hebrew word as a bow for arrows — a war-bow. What a war-bow, spanning the whole horizon! What mighty arrows it must shoot when God goes into battle. "The Lord will march out like a mighty man, like a warrior he will stir up his zeal; with a shout he will raise the battle cry and will triumph over his enemies." (Is 42:12) The rainbow is not a mere phenomenon of beauty but a divine reminder of God's archery. "There was a rainbow round about the throne and out of the throne proceeded lightnings," God's mighty arrows. (Rev 4:3 and 5). No wind can blow a rainbow away. No devil can switch it off. The battle belongs to the Lord. We all suffer life's storms when ominous blackness fills our skies, but that arching splendor of prismatic color in the rain cloud, seen with our mortal eyes, is the objective standard of God to reassure us. God's rainbow is His love bent to the world — and you and me.

SERVITUDE IS NOT SALVATION

Christianity is not all about toiling in the midday sun and burning the midnight oil. Human nature does not measure up to ceaseless grind. Servitude is not salvation. Jesus did not come to tie burdens to people's backs, to stand in constant criticism, imposing stress and anxiety. Adam labored by the sweat of His brow, but Christ expects no such thing of us. He said, "Come to me, all you who labor and are heavy laden, and I will give you rest. Take my yoke upon you and learn from me ... and you will find rest for your souls. For my yoke is easy and my burden is light." (Matt 11:28-30) His call is an opportunity for service; His yoke is a high privilege that sits easily on our shoulders. But He always takes the heavy end of any weight. We are the sons of God, not the sons of toil.

GOD'S LOVE IN ME

Ministry is human personality expressing Christ. The love of God is God's love in me. It is not my love carried by the Holy Spirit, but me carrying His love. We shouldn't ask God to bless our concern for people. We must catch God's concern and let it express itself in our poor humanity. Romans 5:5 tells us that "God has poured out his love into our hearts by the Holy Spirit, who he has given us." I must identify with what God is doing, not ask God to identify with what I am doing. That is a principle of ministry laid down in the New Testament. You and I, we mortals represent Him, His love and mercy must come through our lives not just our mouths. It is by the Christ-life in my life. "We have this treasure in earthen vessels."

OUR SECTOR MAY BE SMALL

Fire demonstrates God's nature but does not explain everything about Him. Fire is more than show, glory, or splendor. It displays His disposition, His infinite greatness, the central source of hope and life in the universe. Our best enthusiasm makes us only a smoldering wick alongside Him, the eternal Sun of Righteousness. Three times we read "The zeal of the Lord will perform this." (2 Kings 19:31, Is 9:7, Is 37:32) That is God. To be His friends we must think big, think worldwide. Our sector may be small, but He puts us where He wants us with allies greater than all the enemy, on the victory front. We are God's sons, commissioned ambassadors, demanding surrender to the King of kings.

SECOND BIBLE

*E*xperience is not a second Bible. We don't check the Bible by our experience. We check our experience by the Bible.

BULLET PROOF

*W*e are told that Napoleon ordered a coat of mail, but he was not quite certain that it was impenetrable, so he said to the manufacturer of that bullet-proof-vest: "Put it on now yourself and let us try it." With shot after shot from his own pistol, the emperor found out that it was first-class quality. Then the man received a large reward. I bless the Lord that the same coat of mail that struck back the weapons of temptation from the heart of Christ in the wilderness *we may now all wear*. Jesus comes and says "I have been tempted, and I know what it is to be tempted. Take this robe that defended me and wear it for yourselves. I shall see you through all trials and I shall see you through all temptations." It's a good deal.

Great
Commission

ISRAEL AND THE WHOLE WORLD

Reading the Bible from the beginning we find ourselves concerned only about *Israel* — book after book, as if God was only the God of the Jews and had limited His interests to that tiny land and small nation. But as soon as we open the New Testament the borders melt away, and the wide *world* comes into view. "For God so loved the *world*..." "Go into all the *world*..." "And they went forth, preaching the Gospel *everywhere*..." The walls of every church should embrace the whole *world*. This is New Testament.

THE GREAT COMMISSION IS FOR ANYBODY

Christ did not give His Great Commission to anybody in particular, nor did he lay down special qualifications. It is a standing invitation to everyone. Godliness and spirituality are wonderful advantages, but they are dormant until Christ's Word "Go!" is obeyed. "Going" launches our spiritual development. It is not an end result. A key word in the Mark's Gospel is "immediately," or "straightway." It occurs over 40 times. It is thought that Peter was behind Mark's Gospel and Peter was himself an "immediate" man, impetuous. Jesus was the man for Peter, for He was also a direct-action personality. The Lord seemed so unhurried, with time for everybody, but He accomplished more in His brief ministry than any man in a lifetime. What a pattern to follow.

NO IMPENDING DEFEAT

Time after time hell engineered events against Christ's birth, but the Word of God stood true, "I will act and who will prevent it?" Pharaoh ordered all Israeli baby boys to be killed but Moses escaped. Haman plotted Israel's genocide, but God had planted Queen Esther in court to prevent it. Little Israel was caught in the nutcrackers of mighty empires but always survived. Even when Jesus was born, Herod sought to destroy him, but God forestalled him. The cross itself seemed the end of all hopes but God had planned it as the greatest triumph of all. In the 21st century Jesus saves, in greater style, greater power, and greater numbers than we ever imagined. God is not struggling with impending defeat but laughing as He moves through the earth doing what no religion or human authority can ever do, changing human beings into the children of God. Our privilege is to come alongside Him as He works. Let's do it together.

NEW SPECIES OF MAN

The apostles were a new species of homo sapiens: spiritual men, the first on earth, new creations in Christ (see 2 Cor 5:17). They were unaffected by the world's opposition in a way no man of the world ever could be. And all that I have said about them holds true for thousands of God's servants around the world today. The same forces are available to every Christian today in the same measure as in the days of the apostles. However great our need, the power of God will be there to meet it. However great the demands of our ministry, the power of God will be there in sufficient measure. But note that there is no such thing as degrees of power — God does not tailor His power to match the degree of our supposed need. Each one of us has all power in Christ. The same resources are freely available to all who serve God (see Jn 3:34 and 1 Cor 12:27).

OUR PLACE IN THE DIVINE PURPOSE

Jesus did not preach sermons in the hope that it would have a good effect generally. He chose people to get on with the task at hand. The Gospels spotlight many very ordinary individuals, even nameless people, and they become keys to spiritual truth. The point to note is this — God not only deals with us as individuals, but He chooses us. He singles us out, just as He singled out Israel. All that God does is important, never insignificant, or incidental. Everything in nature, down to the dancing particles of the atom, moves in accordance with an ultimate divine plan. The whole movement of creation works out the divine will. When we are chosen, it is the direct act of God intervening personally as part of His eternal process. It has that kind of significance. We have a vital place in the divine purpose. Faith puts us there.

WHAT IS GOD SAYING TO THE CHURCH?

People ask, "What is God saying to the church today?" Why is that a problem? Does God speak so inaudibly? He says nothing today that is not in His Word already. I know one thing that God is saying. If our prophets are true, they will be voicing the same urgency as Jesus Christ and echoing the same Great Commission, *"Go ye into all the world and preach the gospel to every creature."*

GOD'S COUNTER-COMMAND

There are plenty of maxims bandied about as if they were Scripture, but they are just popular philosophy, e.g. "Don't move till God tells you" or "Always wait for God." They sound so humble and spiritual, but we search for them in the Bible in vain. Moses himself told the tribes of Israel, "Do not be afraid. Stand firm and you will see the deliverance the Lord will bring you today." (Ex 14:13) God told Moses to stop praying and get off the ground. God gave a counter-command, "Tell the Israelites to move on." (Ex 14:15) God says "Go," the light is green. Let's go for and with Him.

TRIALS?

Trials come, as I know from my own experience. They are like a baking-oven. The heat is atrocious — but the cake is delicious. Enjoy and keep fixing our eyes on Jesus, the author and perfecter of faith (Heb 12:2, NASB)

REFLECTED LIGHT

Jesus said that John was "the burning and shining lamp." (John 5:35) We see this in John 1:5 and 7, where we read, "The light shines in the darkness." John came "to bear witness of the Light." It strikes me that if the light was already shining, why was John needed? When the sun rises, we all know about it — we don't need anybody to testify that it is daylight. So, what is a "witness" of light? If you look into the sky on most clear nights, the moon is shining. Men have been to the moon and they know it generates no light of its own. Also, all space surrounding the moon is void of light. If space is dark and the moon has no light of its own, why is it so bright and how can it bring light to us? We all know, of course, that the moon only reflects light, and that the light comes from the sun.

Well, if the sunlight passes through space to reach the moon, why is space so dark, even near the moon? The answer is very elementary! Light itself is invisible. You only know light is present when it strikes an object. Most of space is completely empty. There is nothing there to catch the light from the sun or hinder the light until it reaches the moon. Space is full of light generated by billions of suns, yet it appears pitch black. The universe is full of God. He is the Father of lights and all light comes from Him. Yet millions walk around in profound darkness. How can that be? How can people walk in spiritual darkness when the whole universe is steeped in the light of God? These people cannot see the light of invisible things until somebody else catches the light and reflects it. The sun's rays would not be seen on earth except for the fact that they illuminate the molecules of our atmosphere, as well as the dust and moisture in the air.

The sun radiates light across billions of miles, and yet there is no trace of it until that light is reflected. We need something to show us it is there. The moon is a witness to the light. It proves that the sun is shining, because it shines with the light of the sun. The moon sails across the sky in invisible sunlight and passes on enough for us to find our way. 1 Timothy 1:17 talks about "the King eternal, immortal, invisible." The light of God is constant, brilliant. It is never intermittent. But who sees it? People walk in darkness. The stark fact is that the only light they will ever see is reflected light. Just as John was a "burning and shining lamp," a witness to the Light, so is every believer. We are commanded to "walk in the light" (1 Jn 1:7), for if we don't, there will be no light. A spiritually lost world depends upon light reflectors. If we hide the gospel, it will remain hidden to those who are lost (see 2 Cor 4:3-6).

LEAVE YOUR COZY ANCHORAGE

It is tragic when believers have no vision and fill in their years without shape or direction. They follow their own fancy, wandering this way or that according to circumstances, leaving no more mark upon the world than a falling leaf. Let the Word speak to their heart! Let the winds of the Spirit fill their sails! They leave their cozy anchorage in the bay, cast off the moorings that bind them to earthly interests, and sail off into the great waters. The Psalm says, "There go the ships" (Ps 104:26) KJV, vessels of divine destiny.

DETONATOR

Evangelism is an explosive, but it needs a detonator — which is prayer. Prayer is a detonator, but it needs an explosive — which is evangelism. Evangelism and intercession are the two feet on which the gospel strides the world.

NO DRY SPOT

God says, "For the earth shall be filled with the knowledge of the glory of the Lord as the waters cover the sea." (Hab. 2:14, KJV) How do the waters cover the sea? So thoroughly that there is not a single dry spot on the bottom of the sea! This clearly illustrates God's plan. The knowledge of His glory, power, and salvation will be spread across the world like a flashflood. There won't be a single dry spot, no ignorant country, city, town, village, family, or individual. "The whole earth is full of His glory" cried the seraphim in Isaiah 6:3.

Marriage

THE HUBBLE TELESCOPE LOOKS FOR STARS — JESUS LOOKS FOR PEOPLE

God's intention is for women to be married. When He made Eve, He married her off straightaway. In fact, she was made to be married. Eve was a made-to-measure, custom-built partner for Adam and Adam was right for her. Neither had problems about whom to marry. They were not offered a selection. He could truly say, "For me you are the only woman in the world," and she could say "You are the only man in the world for me." If a woman wants to be married, she is in partnership with the Lord. *He* wants it that way. God invented marriage and set the pattern. God loves people and all His plans are for their happiness. Whenever His will is done, it makes for happiness like Jesus made wine at Cana and like God made the Garden of Eden for Adam and Eve. The Hubble telescope focuses on the stars, but God focuses on people. One human soul looms bigger in God's eye than Jupiter. A living baby outweighs the dead moon. Our God is love. Praise the Lord.

MARRIAGE WITH SUPER-GLUE

Marriage is God's idea, and it only works as He planned it — with Jesus. Some marriages are not wedlock but padlock. Awful jails! They just make the best of things because they can't escape from one another. Some marriages look okay, like a fine symphony, but it is only on paper, and there's no music. True love comes from God, and marriage is built on it — or collapses. The only glue to hold two people together is love. God's love in their lives is the super-glue. It is the precious blood of Jesus (see Deut 28:8).

GOD AS WEDDING-OFFICIATOR

Creation was the preparation for Adam and Eve's wedding. It would set humanity on its way. I think that is most romantic. The Lord God planned the wedding and then prepared the home. *He* first made the sun and moon for light, set the mighty tides of the ocean in motion, made dry land to appear to provide accommodation for Adam. Then He laid a carpet of green for the first bride and bridegroom to walk upon. It was what the world was made for. God didn't delay His plans. He wanted laughter in the garden. Every wedding is a key idea of God. He is 100 percent behind it. It is part of His scheme to bring all things together in harmony and unity. God brings things together. "Unto Him shall the *gathering* of the people be." (Gen 49:10) He is the gatherer. The devil is the divider and destroyer. We either gather with Christ or scatter with the devil.

MARRIAGE NEEDS GRACE TO PERFECT IT

The perfection is not in cold, legal, dead correctness, but in grace. The ten Commandments are a burden but love and grace are the key. At the marriage of Adam and Eve, God officiated at the wedding. God had said that everything created was "good." But one thing He made was "not good," He said. He said that it was not good for Adam to be alone (see Gen 2:18). His plan was male, and female should make perfection. So, God made Eve. He was happy in what He had made — man and wife. "Good." God created heaven and earth, but the work was not finished until this wedding! Weddings complete God's work, even in heaven! She was

His helpmeet and he was to do the work, she was to help alongside. A perfect marriage is a Christian marriage. Jesus sent out His disciples two-by-two. I think that they were often young married couples working for Jesus. A Christian marriage has a Christian purpose. It spreads the gospel, the love of Jesus, the true picture of what God wants, a world of love.

THE PERFECT COUPLE

The perfect husband is he who doesn't expect his wife to be perfect. The perfect wife is she who doesn't expect her husband to be perfect. But both have a perfect Savior in Jesus Christ.

GOD NOT ONLY LOVES BUT ALSO BLESSES

The purpose of this wedding was to bless the whole world. God said, "I will bless you and in you all families of the earth shall be blessed." The very word family comes 400 times in Scripture. That purpose has come about through the son of Abraham, Jesus (Matt 1:1). Blessing! God not only loves, but also blesses. God's love is not simply a lot of sentiment and a card at Christmas. It is *blessing* — goodness, gifts, care, guidance, and richness. That's the idea. Families are not only the building blocks of a strong society, but they are a pre-condition for the full blessing of God. We *all* begin with family connections in conditions for God's blessing. God *blesses* weddings and wedded couples. They please Him for getting married and qualify for God's blessing.

GOD LIKES WEDDINGS

The Lord God blessed Adam and Eve's wedding in Eden, and Jesus blessed the marriage at Cana by giving them all the wine they needed. (John 2) Both God and God's Son gave weddings priority! Why? Jesus said, "I do always those things which I see the Father do." (Jn 8:29) He had seen the Father at the wedding in Eden, and Christ came to the wedding in Cana. I like weddings because God likes them. He never misses one. The Lord's prayer says, "Thy will be done on earth as it is in heaven." (Matt 6:10) A marriage fulfils God's will, and I am all for that.

SWINGING THE GATES OF HISTORY

The Apostle Paul mingled unnoticed with the crowds on the Roman roads. They never realized that he was swinging the gates of history in Europe. The whole might of the Roman Empire could not resist him. He made converts out of the immoral devotees of the gods and said to them "The time is short. From now on those who have wives should live as if they had none, those who see the things of the world as if they saw them not." (1 Cor 7:29-31) He meant that the limits of time demand that our priorities must be those of the Kingdom of God. The anointed of the Lord are unstoppable. Go for it in the name of Jesus.

References

1   When I survey the Wondrous Cross, Author: Isaac Watts (1707), Public Domain.

2   Look and Live, Author: William A. Ogden (1887), Public Domain.

3   When Peace, Like a River, Author: Horatio Gates Spafford (1873), Tune: VILLE DU HAVRE, Philip P. Bliss (1876).

4   When I survey the Wondrous Cross, Author: Isaac Watts (1707), Public Domain.

5   I Surrender All, Judson W. Van DeVenter, 1896, Public Domain.

6   Attr. John F. Wade (1711-1786); tr. Frederick Oakeley (1802-1880); vss. 2-4 anonymousTune: John F. Wade's Cantus Diversi, 1751, Public Domain.

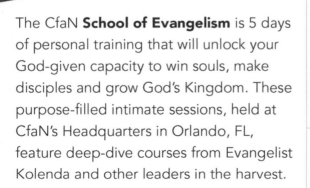